CHICAGO ACES

THE FIRST 75 YEARS

CHICAGO ACES
THE FIRST 75 YEARS

John Freyer and Mark Rucker

ARCADIA

First published 2005

Published by Arcadia Publishing,
Charleston SC, Chicago IL, Portsmouth NH, San Francisco CA

Library of Congress Catalog Card Number: Applied for

For all general information, contact Arcadia Publishing:
Telephone 843-853-2070
Fax 843-853-0044
E-mail sales@arcadiapublishing.com
For customer service and orders:
Toll-free 1-888-313-2665

Visit us on the Internet at www.arcadiapublishing.com

CONTENTS

ACKNOWLEDGMENTS

I'm eternally indebted to Mark Rucker for giving me the chance to share in his world of imagery and his passion for baseball. Thanks again, Mark, for helping me write about baseball.

I'd like to thank Larry Lester for his input on the black players and his unending knowledge of the Negro Leagues.

I'd also like to thank Arcadia's Jeff Ruetsche, for gently prodding me and giving me pointers.

I'd like to mostly thanks Art Ahrens, and the folks at Home Tavern-Chicago, Mike and Katie, for letting me pick Art's mind, a few hours at a time. From the day I met Art, I was amazed by his mental recall of facts, particularly his knowledge of Cubs history. He added colorful anecdotes about the ballplayers and scandalous details of their lives. Art is a true Chicago baseball historian. The stats speak for themselves in this book, the best stories are thanks to Art.

I am indebted to my wife and proofreader extraordinaire, Carrie, and my son, and best friend, Jack, who motivate me, more than they'll ever understand.

And lastly, my little sister Jane, who used to catch me when no one else would.

John Freyer

REFERENCES

Freyer, John and Rucker, Mark, *19th Century Base Ball in Chicago*, Arcadia Publishing, Chicago, Illinois, 2002.

Lester, Larry, Miller, Sammy, and Clark, Dick. *Black Baseball in Chicago*, Arcadia Publishing, Chicago, Illinois, 2000.

The Cubs, Putnam Books, New York, NY 1945.

The Mcmillan Company. *The Baseball Encyclopedia Centennial Edition*, Collier-Macmillan, Toronto, Ontario, Canada 1969.

SABR. *Deadball Stars of the National League*, Brassey's Inc., Dulles, Virginia, 2004.

www.baseball-reference.com
www.baseballhistory.com
www.sabr.org Society for American Baseball Research
www.vintageballist.com
www.ruckerarchive.com

One

1876–1899

Just before the Civil War, in the years of 1859 and 1860, baseball was taking root in Chicago. In 1859, the first recorded game of baseball was played in the city. The Atlantic and Excelsior clubs faced off in a 31 to 17 affair, won by the Excelsior team. The winning pitcher was a Mr. J. Malcolm—the loser, A.L. Adams. Little did they know at the time that they would be regarded as the first known pitchers in Chicago's long history of baseball.

Chicago is steeped in baseball history. It had had one of the first professional teams, the White Stockings of 1870, who are now the Cubs. The National League was formed here in 1876, by Chicago businessman William Hulbert. Charles Comiskey and Clark Griffith of Chicago played a significant role in the development of the American League. Sixteen-inch softball was invented here in the 1890s, by tying a string around a boxing glove, so men could play baseball inside in bad weather. It was then known as "Indoor Baseball." Sixteen inch softball is Chicago's indigenous sport. No other city in the country plays the "Chicago Game."

After the Civil War, the Excelsior club of Chicago was considered the best in the newly developed North-Western Association, which included the Atlantic club of Chicago, along with teams from Detroit, Dubuque, Freeport, and Bloomington, to name a few. A gentleman named Kennedy was the Ace of the 1866 staff that won the Championship of the first association tournament in Rockford, defeating the Empire club of Freeport, 26-24. In 1867, Kennedy gave way to a chap named McNally who became the Ace—until the demise of the Excelsiors after the 1868 season.

In 1869, businessmen in Chicago began to pool their money to draw top players from the East to Chicago, emulating what the Champions of 1869, the Cincinnati Red Stockings, did to put together a team that went 69-0.

In 1870, Chicago introduced the White Stocking club, featuring top of the line pitcher Ed Pinkham, who had pitched for the Brooklyn Eckford club in 1869. The White Stockings were one of the top teams that year, registering a 65-8 record.

In 1871, the National Association was born, the first all professional league. The White Stockings grabbed the services of George Zettlein (He of the Big Feet) from the Brooklyn Atlantics, who had failed to join the new association, because they felt their amateur status was more profitable. The White Stockings were among the elite teams. They lost their home, Lakefront Park, and their uniforms and equipment in the Great Chicago Fire in October, while leading the league. They lost the Championship to the Philadelphia Athletics in a one-game playoff, 4-1. It has been written that the men were homeless and weak from the ordeal of losing all that they had in the Fire.

The team reorganized in 1874, with Zettlein and Jimmy Devlin in the box until 1876, when Hall of Famer Albert Spalding came along and won the inaugural National League Championship. Bringing us up to the outstanding pitchers of the dynastic White Stocking teams of the 1880s . . .

ALBERT GOODWILL "AL" SPALDING
CAREER 1871–1877   CHICAGO 1876–1877

Spalding was the ace pitcher and manager for the first champions of the National League, the 1876 Chicago White Stockings. That season Spalding posted a 46-12 record with a minute 1.75 ERA, pitching a whopping 528 innings. Spalding had a long successful career before the development of the National League. Spalding started pitching at the age of 15 for the Rockford Forest City team in 1866. In 1867, the 16-year-old Spalding was on the mound when the Forest Citys upset the touring Washington Nationals. It was the only loss for the Nationals on the first barnstorming tour of the United States by an organized baseball team. His plaque at the Baseball Hall of Fame proclaims him "Organizational genius of baseball's pioneer days." He was an exceptional pitcher with his straight armed underhand delivery. Spalding was even an accomplished hitter, often hitting in the middle of the lineup as a pitcher. In 1871, he was proclaimed "Champion Pitcher of the World" for the Boston Red Stockings of the old National Association, that predates and was replaced by the National League in 1876. In 1875, Spalding had a 57-5 record for the champion Red Stockings. The arm strain of years as a workhorse took its toll on Spalding. He pitched four games in 1877. He retired at the age of 28, to concentrate on his young sporting goods company, Spalding Sporting Goods, which still exists today. A.G. Spalding and Brothers dominated the sporting good industry in the late 1800s, much like a monopoly. His success as a player enabled him to negotiate full team contracts, and his motto was, "Everything is possible to him who dares." Spalding was the White Stockings team President from 1882 to 1891, during the dynastic years of the White Stockings of the 1880s. He was also the P.T Barnum of baseball, sending his White Stockings on a world tour after the 1888 season, visiting such places as Australia, Hawaii, Egypt, Italy, and England. Spalding was inducted to the Hall of Fame in 1939.

Lawrence "Larry" Corcoran

Larry Corcoran was the most dominant pitcher of the 1880s, before he blew his arm out in 1885 from overuse. Corcoran led the league in victories in 1881 (31) and ERA in 1882 (1.95). He also led the league in strikeouts with 268 in 1880. In his five full seasons with the White Stockings (1880–1884), Corcoran earned 170 wins en route to a sparkling 177-90 career record. He pitched two no-hitters for the White Stockings: August 19, 1880, against the Brooklyn Trolley Dodgers, and June 27, 1884, against the champions of that year, the Providence Greys. He had posted a career ERA of 2.36 with over 1,100 strikeouts. Corcoran was the first pitcher to work out a set of signals with his catcher. Larry always had a wad of chaw in his mouth, so he and catcher Silver Flint figured out a way to communicate based on the position of the chaw in his mouth. The huge amount of chaw could easily be seen by Flint. Bright's disease and dissipation helped end Corcoran's short but mercurial career.

9

JOHN GIBSON CLARKSON

CAREER 1884–1894 CHICAGO 1884–1887

Clarkson had a career 327-177 record with a 2.81 ERA and 1,978 strikeouts. He led the National League in wins in 1885 (53) and 1887 (38) for the White Stockings. He also led in 1888 (33) and 1889 (49) for the Boston Beaneaters. Clarkson was an ace for the pennant winning White Stockings of 1885 and '86. His 53 wins in 1887 are the most ever by a Chicago pitcher, a record that is sure to stand the test of time. Clarkson was inducted to the Hall of Fame in 1963.

Considered a top pitcher in his day, Clarkson was respected by teammates and adversaries alike. Manager Cap Anson proclaimed Clarkson "one of the greatest pitchers," but complained about the ace's perpetual emotional demands, adding "he won't pitch if scolded." Clarkson was generally laid back, but once threw a lemon instead of a ball to prove to an umpire that it was too dark to play. His slow, calculating delivery seemed to intimidate hitters of the day.

Copyright 1887
Goodwin & Co.

Clarkson, P.

John Clarkson is featured on this Old Judge Card, from 1887. Clarkson and King Kelly were sold to the Red Sox in 1888 for $10,000 each, thus ending the White Stocking run of championships in the '80s. He finished his career with the Cleveland Spiders, eventually losing his top pitcher status on the team to a young ace named Cy Young. Clarkson purchased a cigar store after retirement and ran it up until his death at the age of 47.

WILLIAM FORREST "BILL" HUTCHINSON
CAREER 1889–1895, 1897   CHICAGO 1889–1895

"Wild Bill" led the league in victories for some hapless White Stocking/ Colt teams. Hutch won 42 games in 1890, 44 in 1891, and 37 in 1892, also leading the league in strikeouts with 316. Hutch was a former star pitcher at Yale and became the ace for the Colts in the early 1890s. Anson personally signed him after several attempts to pry Hutchinson away from his Iowa farm. After breaking in as a 30-year-old rookie in 1889, Hutchinson posted a 183-162 major league record over his seven seasons with the White Stockings. Wild Bill made an uneventful six-game comeback attempt with St. Louis in 1897.

Clark Calvin "Old Fox" Griffith
Career 1891–1914   Chicago 1893–1902

CLARK C. GRIFFITH

Griffith was a career 236-145 pitcher, winning the bulk of those games in Chicago (152 for the Orphans and 39 for the White Sox). He grew up on the homestead, becoming a professional trapper at the age of 10. The Griffiths moved to Bloomington, Illinois, where he discovered baseball. He signed his first contract in 1888 at the age of 19. In 1893, he garnered a 30-18 record for the Oakland Oaks of the Pacific Coast League. When the Oaks owners refused to disburse back-pay salaries owed to the players, Griffith organized a strike. To find pay in the interim, he and several teammates went on the vaudeville circuit around San Francisco. The owners eventually found some money, and the season was finished. Griffith was signed by Cap Anson in 1893. He was called the "Old Fox" due to the fact he had six pitches in his repertoire, including the screwball, which Griffith always claimed he invented. Griffith also utilized the quick pitch and hid the ball well with his body before throwing, possibly the first pitcher to use this deception. Griffith scuffed, scratched, cut and spit on nearly every pitch he ever threw. The Old Fox won 20-plus games for the sub-par Chicago National League club six times in a row between 1894 and 1899. Griffith posted a 21-14 record in 1894, 26-14 in 1895, 23-11 in 1896, 21-18 in 1897, 24-10 in 1898, and 22-14 in 1899. His 1.88 ERA led the National League in 1898. Griffith went 24-7 with a 2.67 ERA for the pennant winning White Sox of 1901. He was inducted to the Hall of Fame in 1946.

Clark Griffith had a lot to do with the organization of the American League. In 1900, he led members of the Player's Association to baseball's first strike, over raising the salary to $3,000 and not having the players pay for their own uniforms. Griffith persuaded 39 National League stars to jump to the American League. He was rewarded by getting the player/manager position for the 1901–1902 White Sox, before taking on the same role for the New York Highlanders (Yankees) in 1903. In 1911, American League President Ban Johnson begged Griffith to take over the struggling Washington franchise, and there Griffith blossomed into his lifelong role of running the Senators. Griffith's main innovation to the game was the development of the relief pitcher as a manager of the Washington Senators. Firpo Marberry was used exclusively as a reliever, particularly if Walter Johnson was tiring. Marberry's side arm delivery was the perfect compliment to Johnson's powerful fastball. Griffith discovered the effectiveness of changing pitchers during the 1924 World Series against John McGraw and the New York Giants.

John W. "Jack" Taylor
Career 1898–1907   Chicago 1898-1903, 1907

Jack Taylor, a career 150-139 pitcher, had a 1.33 ERA to lead the National League in 1902, sporting a 22-11 record. He followed that up in 1903 with a 21-14 record and a 2.48 ERA. Taylor was a workhorse, pitching 187 consecutive complete games from 1901 to 1906. He had an uncanny knack of getting National League star Honus Wagner out. "Had Wagner been obliged to bat against Old Jack Taylor all through a season his average would have shrunk to .150," once quipped Ed Reulbach, Taylor's teammate and fellow pitcher. Taylor was a crafty control pitcher, nibbling on the corners and changing speeds.

ROY LEWIS PATTERSON
CAREER 1901–1907   CHICAGO 1901-1907

Patterson posted a career 82-69 with a 2.75 ERA. "The Saint Croix Boy Wonder" came onto the scene after beating Charles Comiskey's St. Paul Saints team in the Western League in 1898. In 1900, when the Saints would be moved to Chicago and become the Sox, Patterson was the best pitcher on the club. The Boy Wonder was on the mound for the new American League's first game, on April 24, 1901, beating the Cleveland Blues, 8-2. The Sox won the first pennant with Patterson going 20-16 with a 3.37 ERA. He, along with Clark Griffith and Nixey Callahan, gave the White Sox a formidable rotation. Patterson ha a fine sophomore year as well, going 19-14 with a 3.06 ERA. After leaving Major League ball in 1907,Patterson played for the minor league Minneapolis Millers for another decade.

18

James Joseph "Nixey" Callahan
Career 1894–1913 Chicago 1897–1903

Callahan was a career 99-73 pitcher with a lifetime 3.39 ERA who split time between the mound, outfield, and infield. "Nixey" and Clark Griffith were the first pitchers to play for both the Cubs and the White Sox. Both pitchers were successful for the Cubs of the late 1800s and the Sox in the first few years of their existence. Nixey was on the mound when the Cubs put up 36 runs against Louisville in 1897. The Cubs won the game, 36-7, still a National League record for runs in a single game. Callahan's best years were with the Orphans when he went 20-10 with a 2.46 ERA in 1898, and 21-12 with a 3.06 ERA in 1899. He followed his success up with the Orphans by going 15-8 with a 2.42 ERA in 1901 for the pennant winning White Sox of the American League. He went 16-14 with a 3.60 ERA in 1902 for the Sox. Nixey pitched the first no-hitter for the White Sox franchise, on September 20, 1902, versus the Detroit Tigers. He pitched the no-hitter the day after his bachelor party with a horrible hangover. Callahan was player-manager for the White Sox in 1903 and turned the reigns over to Fielder Jones in 1904; he played, but never pitched again after that.

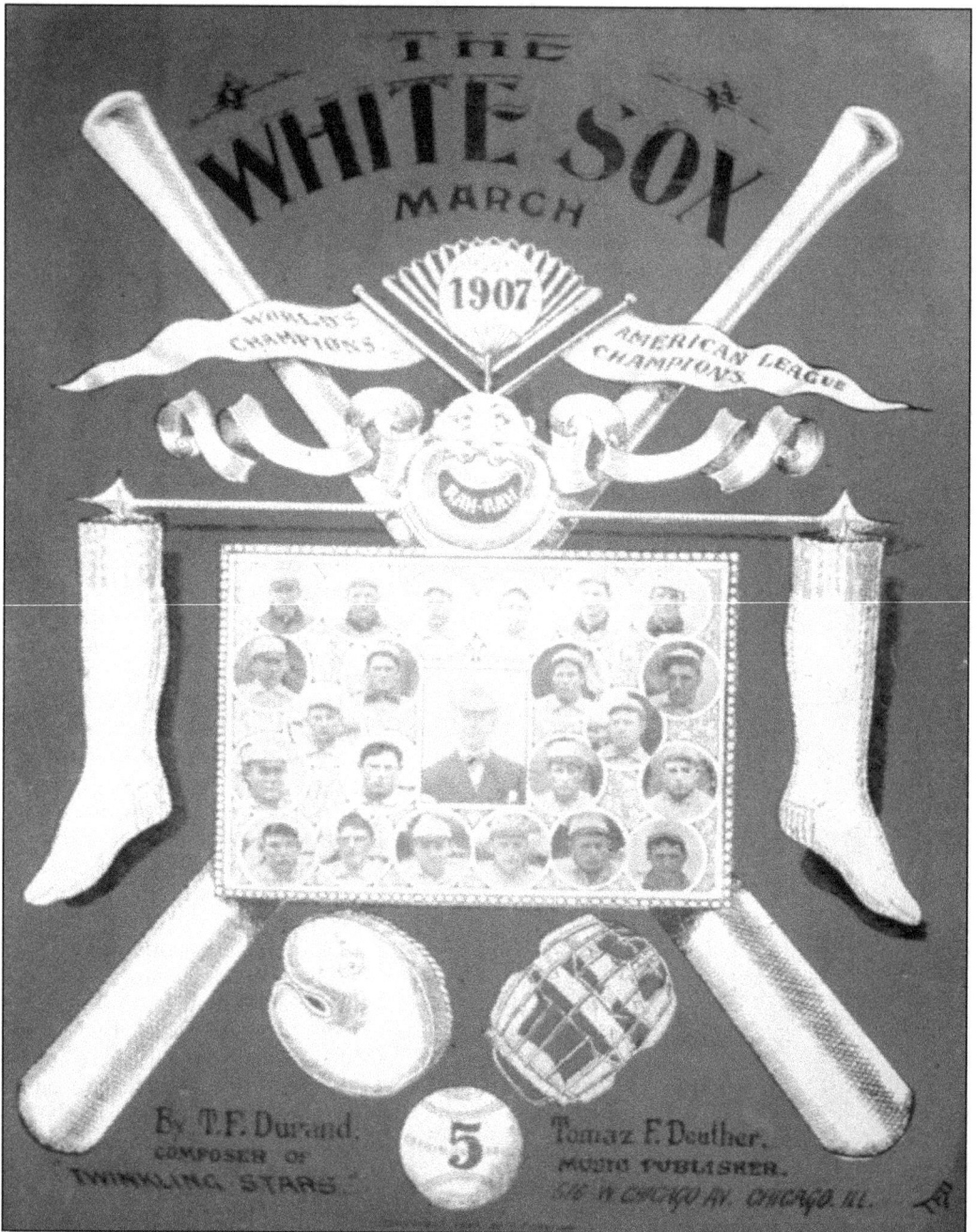

This 1907 printed sheet music features the World Champion White Sox. "The Hitless Wonders," coached by Fielder Jones, hit an anemic .230 during the 1906 season, but tight pitching helped them during the season and the World Series. Among the aces on the staff were Ed Walsh (17-13), Doc White (18-6), Frank Owen (22-13), and Nick Altrock (20-13).

Guy Harris "Doc" White
Career 1901–1913   Chicago 1903-1913

"Doc" was a career 185-155 pitcher with a 2.38 ERA and 1,384 strikeouts. Doc White and Ed Walsh anchored a right-left combination for a decade. The Sox were a no-hit, good-field, strong-pitching team. The 1906 Hitless Wonder were only successful because of their strong pitching. White led the American League that year with a 1.52 ERA, while posting a 18-6 record. He followed that season up a 25-13 and a 2.26 ERA campaign in 1907. Doc had double digit victories in each of the next four years: 18-13 in 1908, 11-9 in 1909, 15-13 in 1910, and 11-15 in 1911.

In his World Series appearances in 1906, White went 1-1 in with a minuscule 1.80 ERA. Doc White got the nickname because he was a dentist in the off season. He was a graduate of Georgetown College of Dental Surgery. In September of 1904, he threw five shutouts in a row, the streak ending when he pitched both ends of a double header. Doc had pinpoint control. He set an early American League record for not allowing a walk over 65 innings.

White was also an accomplished violinist, balladeer, and songwriter. He wrote, with Ring Lardner, "A Little Puff of Smoke, Goodnight," a best seller in its day. He coached a college team after his playing days were over, owned a Texas League baseball franchise, and became a traveling evangelist later in his life.

Andrew "Rube" Foster
Career 1902–1926 Chicago American Giants

Foster was an outstanding pitcher, a shrewd manager, and the dominant force behind the growth of black baseball in America. New York Giants manager, John McGraw, saw Foster play for the Yellow Jackets, a traveling black team from Texas. He tried to get Foster and other black pitchers to join the Giants, but under the rules of the day wasn't able to use them. Instead, McGraw had Foster tutor his pitchers. Supposedly, it was Foster that taught Christy Mathewson his famous "fadeaway," a screwball. Foster soon joined the Chicago Union Giants in 1902, pitching a shutout in first start. He honed his skills for a white team in the Michigan State league, before ending up with the Cuban Giants later in 1902. Because of uneven statistics for Negro League games, Foster's pitching career is part myth and part fact. He is credited with a 51-4 season early in his career. There is no documentation of a no-hitter he threw in 1904, against Camden, N.J. It is believed that he got the name nickname "Rube," by beating Rube Waddell in a game in 1902. Frank Chance said Foster was the most polished pitcher he ever saw in the box. Honus Wagner said Foster was the greatest pitcher he ever saw. Foster began managing in 1907 for the Leland Giants, guiding them to 110-10 record. Their record was 64-21-1 in 1908. In 1909, Foster challenged the pennant winning Cubs to a series, which the Cubs won in three close games. Foster pitched the second game and took a 5-2 lead into the ninth inning, but lost 6-5. Three Finger Brown won the first and third contests. Foster was inducted to the Hall of Fame in 1981.

CARL LEONARD LUNDGREN
CAREER 1902–1909   CHICAGO 1902-1909

Lundgren was a 90-53, 2.42 ERA career pitcher. He won 10 games plus for five years in a row for the top Cub teams of the early 1900s. He won 18 games for the pennant winners in 1907, posting a 1.17 ERA. Carl also won 17 in 1904 and again in 1906. Though Lundgren pitched well during the year, something always happened to him just enough to keep him out of the World Series. He was a University of Illinois grad who came to the Cubs straight from college. After his playing days were over, Lundgren went back to his alma mater to coach the baseball team.

Mordecai Peter Centennial "Three Finger" Brown
Career 1903–1916 Chicago 1904–1912, 1915–1916

Brown had a lifetime record of 229-131, earning 117 wins over several seasons with the Cubs and adding 18 more on the mound for the 1915 Chicago Whales of the upstart Federal League. The "Miner" led the National League with an ERA of 1.04 in 1906. Brown was the main pitcher of the fabled Tinker-to-Evers-to Chance teams of the 1900s, winning 20 or more games for the Cubs five times during their heyday: 1906 (25), 1908 (27), 1909 (26), 1910 (21), and 1911 (20). He appeared in four World Series with the Cubs (1906, '07, '08, and 1910) posting a career 5-4 record with a 2.81 ERA in the big games. Four out of five of Brown's World Series wins were shutouts. His career ERA of 2.06 is still third best all-time. He is also eighth on the list for major league shutouts with 56. Brown was elected to the Hall of Fame in 1949.

Three Fingers Brown turned his handicap into a "twirler's hand." When Brown was seven, his arm got stuck in a corn grinder at his uncle's farm. They had to amputate almost all the forefinger, and although not severed, his middle finger was mangled and left crooked. His little finger was also a stub. The newspapers called him "Three Finger," though his teammates called him "Miner" due to the fact that he worked in a coal mine before playing baseball at age 24. He started as an infielder until he learned he could make the ball spin by twirling it off of a stub of a finger. Mordecai was one of the most dominant pitchers of his day, along with Christy Mathewson of the New York Giants. Their classic marquee match-ups were stuff of legends. Brown was always matched up against Christy Mathewson and bettered "Matty" on half of the occasions. After Matty threw a no-hitter against Brown in 1905, Miner ran off nine consecutive victories against his old arch nemesis—the ninth coming in the playoff game decided by the famous "Merkle's Boner." In 1916, they faced each other for the last time, each with 12 wins against the other. Mathewson won that day, in what turned out to be the last game for each pitcher. Brown was always a strong pitcher and in 1914 *American Monthly*, a national magazine, published photos of his exercise program, a rugged series of body building routines.

26

John Theodore Joseph "Jack" Pfiester

Career 1903–1911   Chicago 1906–1911

"Jack the Giant Killer" gained that moniker by his ability to tame the John McGraw-led New York Giants. Pfiester had a career 15-5 record against the rival Giants. His lifetime record was 70-45, earning 69 of those wins while in a Cubs uniform. Pfiester came to the Cubs from the Pirates before the 1906 season. Having only won one game before 1906, Jack put up a 19-9 record with a 1.56 ERA in his first full season as a Cub. He followed that up by leading the National League with a 1.15 ERA in 1907. It is the fifth lowest single-season ERA in the history of baseball. Pfiester pitched on four World Series bound Cubs teams, going 1–3 in five starts.

Edward Victor "Eddie" Cicotte
Career 1905–1920   Chicago 1912–1920

Eddie Cicotte was a career 207-147 pitcher with a 2.37 ERA and 1,374 strikeouts. He would be in the Hall of Fame were it not for his role in the 1919 Black Sox Scandal, throwing the World Series. Eddie was in his prime as a pitcher when the scandal hit. The fact that the Sox won the Pennant in 1917 and 1919 had a lot to do with Cicotte's pitching. Eddie led the American League in victories in 1917 (28) and 1919 (29). He also pitched a no-hitter on April 14, 1917, versus the St. Louis Browns. This was probably due to his use of "shine ball," a pitch used before the spitter was outlawed. Though not technically a "spit ball," the shine ball was still a deceiving pitch. The pitcher would melt paraffin wax on the inside of his uniform pants, so not to tip off the umpires, and then rub the waxed spot on his uniform pants. This gave the ball better traction for a tighter spin. Cicotte was declared ineligible in 1920 by Judge Landis along with the other White Sox conspirators. Eddie went 21-10 with a 3.26 ERA in his last season (1920). The only time he "beat himself," he was paid $10,000 to do it. Though he took the bribe, Eddie was not a disgruntled player. He was unhappy with his salary as his career wound down and wanted the money to buy a farm. "I did it for my wife and kiddies," he later explained. He worked at Ford in Detroit for many years before he could actually retire.

Frank Elmer Smith (born Schmidt)
Career 1904–1915   Chicago 1904–1910

"Nig" had a nice string of seasons for the White Sox in the early 20th Century. Smith posted a 23-11 mark in 1907 and a nifty 2.47 ERA. Nig had another stellar season in 1909, when he rejoined the team after skipping out in 1908. Smith went 24-17 and had a tiny 1.80 ERA. Nig Smith pitched two no hitters for the Sox. The first came on September 6, 1905, against the Detroit Tigers. The second was on September 20, 1908, against the Philadelphia Athletics.

Two

1900–1930

With the birth of the American League, the player pool seemed to be evenly spread across both leagues. The White Sox were fortunate enough to import pitchers like Hall of Famer Clark Griffith and Nixey Callahan from the Chicago Orphans (soon to be Cubs). They immediately won the first American League Pennant in 1901. The World Series was still a couple of years off, first appearing in 1903.

By 1906, the Sox had built a strong rotation featuring Hall of Famer Ed Walsh, with Nick Altrock and Doc White. That same year, the young "Cubs" were putting together a dynastic five-year run of great teams. But 1906 was the Sox year, besting the Cubs four games to two in the World Series, behind strong pitching on both sides.

The Cubs returned to the World Series the next year behind Hall of Famer "Three Finger" Brown, Orval Overall, Ed Reulbach, and Jack "The Giant Killer" Pfiester. The Cubs beat Ty Cobb's Detroit Tigers four games to none, with one tie, in a five-game Series. Cubs pitchers held the potent Tiger offense to nine runs in the five games.

The Cubs returned in 1908 to best the Tigers again with a 4-1 Series victory—sadly the last Championship for the Cubs. The Cubs took one more shot at the title in 1910 with the same staff, falling short to Chief Bender and Jack Coombs, four games to one.

During this period the Leland Giants, featuring Ace pitcher Hall of Famer Rube Foster, was tearing up the country as a barnstorming team. In the early 1900s, Frank Leland bought the Page Fence Giants from Adrian, Michigan and brought them to Chicago. Under the tutelage of Rube Foster, the Leland Giants posted an amazing 110-10 mark in 1908. Foster eventually bought the team from Leland and changed the name to the Chicago American Giants, a team that would win several Negro National League Championships in the 1920s and last until the mid-40s, when black players were finally allowed to play in the Major Leagues.

The White Sox of the late 'teens received a boost when the A's sold off Hall of Famer Eddie Collins and the Indians sold off the infamous Joe Jackson to the White Sox. The added offense and stellar pitching kept the Sox competitive from 1915 to 1920, when eight players—including pitchers Eddie Cicotte and Lefty Williams—were suspended for life for their roles in the 1919 Black Sox Scandal. The 1917 staff won the Series from the highly favored New York Giants four games to two, behind stellar pitching from Hall of Famer Urban Faber and Eddie Cicotte.

On the Northside, the Cubs made a run at the World Series in 1918, behind the pitching of Hippo Vaughn and Lefty Tyler, but were beat by a young pitcher named Babe Ruth and the Boston Red Sox. Ruth and Carl Mays dominated the Series, leading Boston to the Championship, four games to two.

The Cubs put a World Series team on the field in 1929, only to lose to the Philadelphia Athletics, four games to one, in a Series that saw the Cubs staff blow a 8-0 lead in the seventh inning of Game Four. They lost Game Five, 3-2, after leading 2-0 going into the bottom of the ninth. Charlie Root, Pat Malone, and Guy Bush were the Aces of the staff that year.

1905 Chicago Leland Giants

Frank Leland (#8) and his Leland Giants were an unstoppable barnstorming force. Besides playing the black teams in Chicago and the Midwest, they would travel through the states

playing small town clubs. In 1908, they posted a record of 110-10.

Edward Augustine "Ed" Walsh
Career 1904–1917   Chicago 1904–1916

"Big Ed" was one the best pitchers in the American League from 1906 to 1912. Walsh's career ERA of 1.82 is the lowest of all time. Walsh had a rocket arm and led the American League in strikeouts in 1908 (269) and 1910 (255). Walsh had an amazing 40 wins over a hearty 464 innings to lead the league in 1908. No pitcher has won as many games in a single season since. He also led the league in losses in 1910 with 20, posting a 16-20 record. He again led the league in losses in 1911, though Walsh had a record of 26-18. Ed attributed his durability to his best pitch, the spitball, which was easy on his arm. Before playing ball, Walsh drove a mule team for a coal mine in Pennsylvania. He was discovered by Charles Comiskey while playing in the minor leagues for Newark, N.J. His stellar ERAs led the major leagues in 1907 (1.60) and 1910 (1.27). Big Ed pitched a no-hitter on August 27, 1911, against the Boston Red Sox. His 57 career shutouts rank sixth all-time. Ed Walsh was in his first full season with the White Sox in 1906 and helped elevate them to the American League pennant that year going 19-15 with a 1.88 ERA. He won his two World Series games that year against the Cubs, posting a 1.80 ERA. Walsh struck out 12 batters in Game Three, blanking the Cubs on two hits. He suffered from a sore arm in 1913 and was never the same again. Sox manager Fielder Jones had Walsh room with journeyman pitcher, Elmer Stricklett, to learn the mysteries of the spitball. Walsh threw a two-hitter in his next outing after learning the pitch. Walsh was inducted to the Hall of Fame in 1946.

Walsh threw every other day for the Sox during his iron-man years. He soon began to feel the abuse in 1909, throwing only half the innings he did in 1908. After winning 27 games in 1911 and 1912, Walsh pitched less than 100 innings in 1913. By 1916, his arm was dead. He came back briefly with the Braves after a year off and was released after 18 innings. He umped in American League in 1922 and eventually went on to coach in the Eastern League and later became a pitching coach for the White Sox for a decade.

WILLIAM "KID" GLEASON
MANAGER WHITE SOX 1919–1923

Kid Gleason (pictured from left to right are Ed Walsh, Kid Gleason, and Nixey Callahan) was best known as the manager of the 1919 Black Sox. Kid was also a decent pitcher in his day for the Pittsburgh Pirates, St. Louis Cardinals, and Baltimore Orioles of the 1890s. He had a career 138-130 record with a 3.79 ERA. When they moved the mound back to its modern distance in 1894, Gleason became ineffective and switched to second base, where he helped the National League Baltimore Orioles win a pennant in 1895. According to some reports, Kid was the first manager to order an intentional base on balls as a strategy to bypass strong hitters. Gleason was nicknamed "Kid" in part due his 5-foot-7 stature, but mostly due to his enthusiasm. He had his heart broken by his players involved in the 1919 scandal. After coaching the crippled teams in the aftermath of the Scandal until 1923, Kid Gleason went on to coach for Connie Mack and the A's through the 1920s and '30s.

ORVAL OVERALL
CAREER 1905–1913   CUBS 1906–1913

Overall's career 2.24 ERA is the eighth lowest of all time. A sore arm hurt his career in 1910, after several dominant seasons for the dynastic pennant winning Cubs of the early 1900s. Orval came from Cincinnati in mid-season 1906 and made a definite impact, going 12-3 for the Cubs during their pennant drive. He followed that up, leading the National League in wins in 1907 with a 23-7 record and a 1.70 ERA. For the 1908 pennant winners, he was 17-11 with a 1.92 ERA. He also dominated the Tigers in the World Series that year, going 2-0 with a 0.98 ERA for the Cubs—their most recent championship. Overall came back with a 21-11 season in 1909 with a 1.42 ERA and 205 strikeouts to lead the league. He appeared in a total of four World Series, pitching in eight games. His record for the Series was 3-1 with a 1.58 ERA, one of the best for a Chicago pitcher in the post season. He beat the Tigers once in 1907, and twice in 1908, including a Series clinching three-hit shut out in Game 5. He also struck out four men in the first inning. That remains a World Series record to this day. A sore arm in 1910 led to Overall getting brutalized in his World Series start, giving up three runs in three innings. He was out of baseball by the end of 1913.

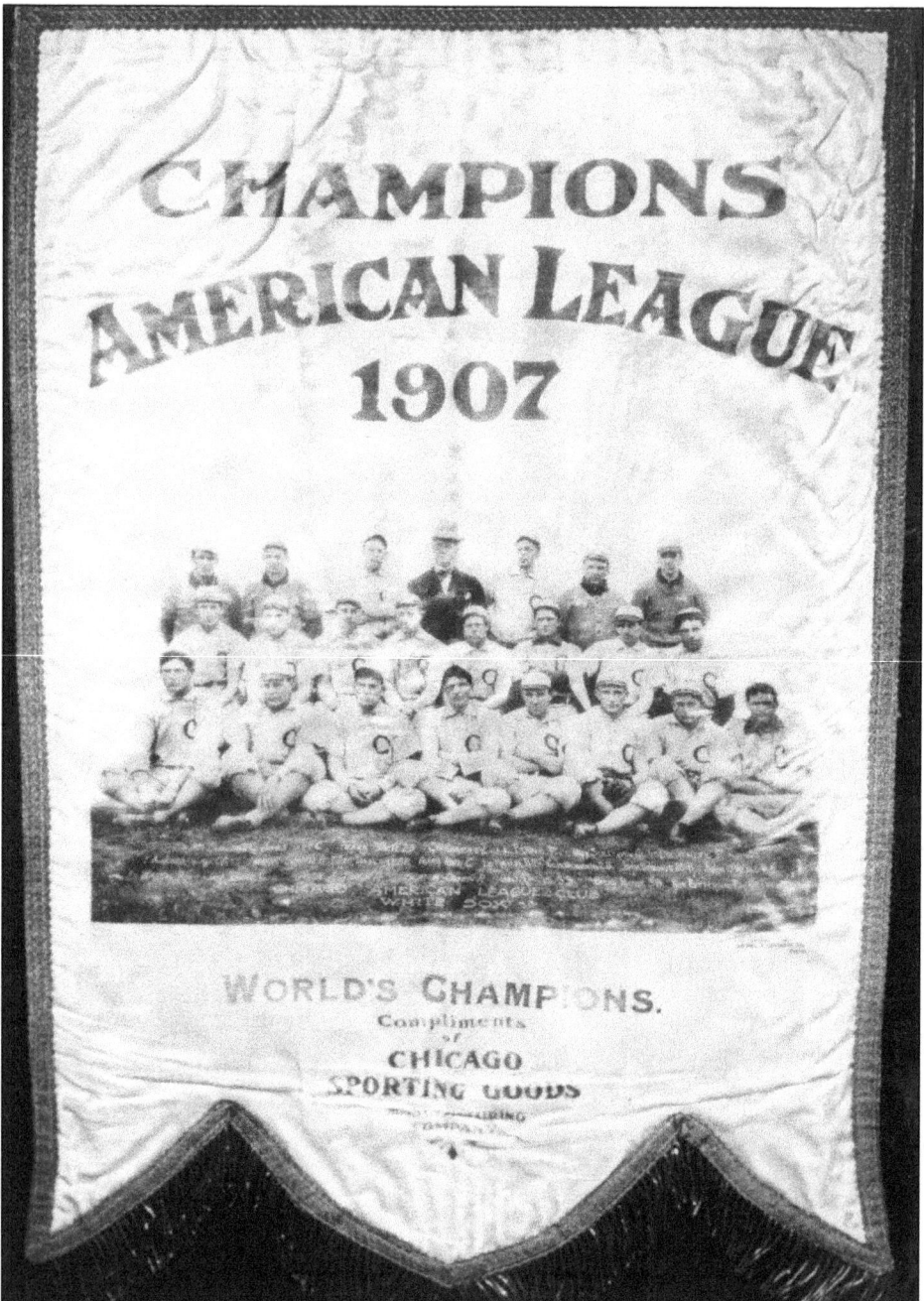

This is the 1907 banner for the 1906 Champions. The Sox hit .198 in the World Series, but the Cubs hit .196. The Sox won the Series four games to two. There was stellar pitching on each side of town. Ed Walsh and Three Finger Brown were the featured baseball idols of their day—Walsh from the Southside and Brown the Northside.

EDWARD MARVIN "ED" REULBACH
CAREER 1905–1917   CHICAGO 1905–1913

"Big Ed" had an immediate impact on the National League when he joined the Cubs in 1905. Reulbach went 18-14 with a 1.42 ERA his rookie season, following that up with a 20-4, 1.65 ERA season for the 1906 pennant winners. His best season was 1908, when he posted a 24-7 record and a 2.03 ERA. His career 2.28 ERA is eleventh best all-time. Big Ed pitched in four World Series for the early powerhouse Cubs, going 2-0 in seven games with a 3.03 ERA. He pitched a one-hitter against the White Sox in the 1906 Series. Reulbach is the only pitcher in history to throw a double-header shutout. He accomplished the feat on September 26, 1908, against the Brooklyn Superbas (Dodgers). Big Ed had bad eyes, so his catchers would put white paint on their gloves so he could see the target. He set the still-standing record of leading the National League in win percentage for a three year span from 1906 to 1908, with records of 19-4, 17-4, and 24-7. He was 140-64 as a Cub. Reulbach took a back seat to Mordecai Brown and cross-town idol Ed Walsh for notoriety, always overshadowed by their accomplishments.

James Leslie "Hippo" Vaughn
Career 1908–1921   Cubs 1913–1921

Hippo Vaughn was one of most dominant pitchers of the National League between 1914 and 1920. He went 150-104 as a Cub. In 1918, a year the Cubs won the pennant, he won the pitching Triple Crown, leading in the top three categories (a 22-10 record, a 1.74 ERA, and 148 strikeouts). Vaughn averaged twenty wins a season for the seven years spanning 1914 to 1920. In his dominant years Hippo put up the following numbers:
21-13, 2.05 ERA (1914), 19-12, 2.87 ERA (1915), 17-14, 2.20 ERA (1916), 23-13, 2.01 ERA (1917), 22-10, 1.74 ERA (1918), 21-14, 1.79 ERA (1919), and 19-16, 2.54 ERA (1920). Vaughn pitched well in the World Series in 1918, though his record doesn't reflect it. He went 1-2 in three starts, posting a sensational 1.00 ERA. Vaughn pitched one of the most unique games in history. On May 2, 1917, Vaughn faced Cincinnati Red, Fred Toney, in one of the greatest pitching duels of all time. The game was tied after nine innings with both pitchers throwing no-hitters. With one out in the tenth inning, Vaughn gave up two hits and lost, 1-0, as Toney completed his no-hitter in his half of the tenth.

40

LEWIS A. "LEW" RICHIE
CAREER 1906–1913 CHICAGO 1910-1913

Richie came over from the Boston Beaneaters in 1910, going 12-4 for the Cubs pennant winners of that year. Lew followed that up with two 16-win seasons in 1911 and 1912. He did pitch in one World Series game in 1910, throwing a scoreless inning in his only appearance. Richie was also said to have been the inspiration behind many of Ring Larder's humorous stories. Richie, a pantomimist, often fell in with Lardner's pranks to pass the time on long train trips.

Leonard Leslie "King: Cole

Career 1909–1915 Chicago 1909-1912

King Cole had one of the best first seasons for a pitcher ever. After pitching in one game for the 1909 Cubs, King Cole went on to go 21-4 with a 1.80 ERA in his first full season in 1910, numbers that rarely are approached by rookies of any era. He followed that up with a 18-7 record and a 3.13 ERA in 1911. Cole also pitched one game in the 1910 World Series, getting a no decision and posting a 3.38 ERA in the big game. Cole's 41-13 record for the Cubs is one of the best winning percentages in the history of the team. King Cole died of cancer at the young age of 29 in 1916.

Ring Larder immortalized Cole by writing about him in his articles in the *Sporting News*, which later emerged as Alibi Ike stories. According to Lardner, the slow-thinking Cole was a horrible poker player and was once threatened by manager Frank Chance with a fine of $50 for spoiling poker games on train trips.

GEORGE ALBERT "LEFTY" TYLER
CAREER 1910–1921   CHICAGO 1918–1921

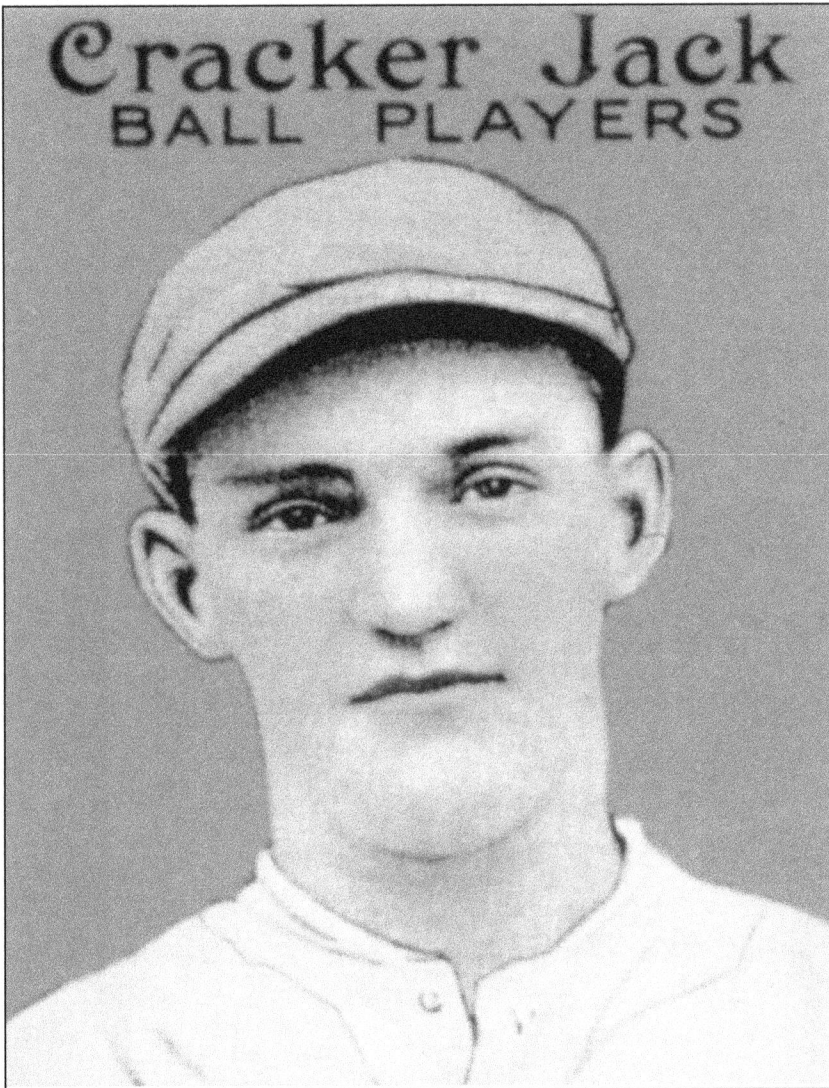

Hard throwing "Lefty" came to the Cubs in 1918 and helped secure the pennant that year with a 19-9 record. He also had a sparkling 2.00 ERA. He only won another 16 games over the next three seasons after his first season as a Cub. Lefty had a good World Series, going 1-1 with a 1.17 ERA in three Series starts against the Boston Red Sox. He took Game Two, 3-1, on a six-hitter, and hit a two-run single to help win the game. He took a tough no-decision in Game Four, giving up two runs and three hits in seven innings. In the deciding Game Six, Tyler lost 2-1 with two unearned runs. Tyler won a 2-1, 21-inning game against the Phillies in 1918, scattering 13 hits and walking just one batter. A sore arm sidelined him 1919, and he lasted one more full season. Tyler umpired in the minors for 12 years after leaving pro ball. He was known as a prankster, often shooting toothpicks and buckshot through his rolled up tongue at the players in the dugout or at their wives at social functions.

JOSEPH LOUIS "JOE" BENZ
CAREER 1911–1919   CHICAGO 1911–1919

"Blitzen" spent his whole career with the White Sox. Benz won 15 games in 1914 and again in 1915. He had the dubious distinction of leading the American League in losses in 1914 (19). Benz had a good spitter and knuckleball. In 1914, despite three errors, he no-hit the Indians, 6-1. He followed that up by two-hitting the Highlanders (Yankees), and then no-hitting Walter Johnson's Washington Senators for eight innings. In the ninth, Eddie Ainsmith hit a roller towards Buck Weaver at short, third baseman Scotty Alcock stuck out his glove and deflected the ball into the outfield, spoiling the no-hitter. This amazing three-game stretch, occurred in a season that Benz lost 19 games.

GROVER CLEVELAND "PETE" ALEXANDER
CAREER 1911–1930 CHICAGO 1918–1926

Alexander had difficulty with almost everything in life except for pitching. He was a solitary man who barely spoke in his whisper-like voice. His teammate and his longtime personal catcher, Reindeer Bill Killefer, was his best friend. Alexander wouldn't accept a trade to the Cubs without bringing Killefer along with him. His alcoholism was well known before Ronald Reagan portrayed him as a pitching drunk in *The Winning Team*. Despite rumors of pitching drunk and with hangovers, alcohol didn't affect him until late in his career. He also suffered from epilepsy, which may have been mistaken as drunken behavior. The disease first appeared during his military service in France. It affected his equilibrium and also affected his hearing after that. Some say the injury could have occurred many years before while playing minor league baseball in Galesburg, Illinois. He took a relay to first, square in the head, while trying to break up a double play. In a coma for two days, Pete awoke with double vision. Alexander had a shambling walk and his uniform never seemed to fit right. His hat looked too small for his head, but he was graceful on the mound. His pitching motion was effortless, his stride short, his delivery three quarters and his arm appeared to disappear into his shirt when he pitched. He had a live fastball and a sharp curve and changed speeds on both. He lived on the low outside corner of the plate. When Alexander was 40, he got his best contract ever—$17,000—and he responded with 21 wins in 1927. Whiskey and age caught up to him, and he pitched on demeaning barnstorming teams until he was 51.

46

"Pete" was a career 374-208 pitcher with a 2.56 ERA and 2,199 strikeouts. He led the National League in victories with the Phillies in 1911 (28), 1914 (27), 1915 (31), 1916 (33), 1917 (33), and with the Cubs in 1920 (27). Alexander also led all pitchers in ERA with the Phillies in 1915 (1.22), 1916 (1.55), 1917 (1.86), and with the Cubs in 1919 (1.72) and 1920 (1.91). He led the league in strikeouts for the Phillies in 1912 (1915), 1914 (214), 1915 (241), 1916 (167), 1917 (201), and with the Cubs in 1920 (173). Alexander's 374 wins is still third highest all-time, behind Cy Young and Walter Johnson. His 88 shut outs rank second on the all-time list behind Walter Johnson. Pete also was been in the Top 10 of Games Pitched (10th), Games Started (7th), Innings Pitched (5th) and Hits Allowed (5th). Alexander's best year with the Cubs was 1920. He went 27-14 with a 1.91 ERA and 173 strikeouts, all of which led the league the pitcher's Triple Crown. Pete led the National League in seven pitching categories that season. Alexander won two games for the St. Louis Cardinals in the 1926 World Series, when the Cubs traded him in mid-season after a suspension. Though Alexander had some success with the Cubs, he missed the 1918 Series due to Military Service. His stellar season in 1920 was for a sub .500 team (75-79). He was inducted to the Hall of Fame in 1938.

47

David Charles "Dave" Danforth

Career 1911–1925   Chicago 1916–1919

"Dauntless Dave," at 27-38, may appear to have a mediocre White Sox record, but Danforth was essentially the first real bullpen ace for the Sox. Danforth led the American League in wins by a reliever with nine in 1917, and again with six in 1918. Dauntless Dave also led the league with seven saves in 1917. Danforth was a key cog in the wheel of the pennant winning machine of 1917, going 15-6 with 2.65 ERA, primarily as a reliever. He led the American League in game appearances by a pitcher with 50 in 1917. He did appear in one World Series game but was beat up in relief, giving up two runs in his only inning. He was called Dauntless Dave because he pitched through the constant pain in his left arm. Danforth used his strong hands to loosen the covers of the balls to help his curveball.

GEORGE NEELY McCONNELL
CAREER 1909–1916   CHICAGO 1914—1916

McConnell had a whopper of a season in 1915 for the Federal League's Chicago Whales. George went 24-10 that season with a 2.20 ERA, the only winning season of his career. This stellar year was sandwiched between a couple of mediocre seasons with the Cubs. McConnell was a first baseman before becoming a spitball pitcher. McConnell won 30 games for the Triple-A Rochester club of the International League in 1913.

James Sanford "Jimmy" Lavender

Career 1912–1917   Chicago 1912-1916

The spitballing Jimmy Lavender had a solid rookie season in 1912, going 15-13 with a 3.04 ERA. That was his only winning season as a Cub. He was the winning pitcher to break Rube Marquardt's 19-game winning streak in 1912. Lavender was also a reputed spitball pitcher. On August 31, 1915, he pitched a no-hitter against the New York Giants.

Victor Eddington "Vic" Aldridge
Career 1917–1928   Chicago 1917–1924

Vic Aldridge had three 15-plus win seasons for the Cubs in the early 1920s. Aldridge's best year was 1923, when he won 16 and lost nine with a 3.48 ERA. Vic won two games in the 1925 World Series for the Pittsburgh Pirates. He also pitched for the 1927 Pirates team that faced the Yanks in the Series. Vic Aldridge went on to become a State Senator in Indiana.

WASHINGTON PARK, 1912

The Cubs are seen here playing in Washington Park in Brooklyn in 1912. Mordecai Brown is pitching and in his follow through watches the batter pop up. Johnny Evers is at 2nd base and

Joe Tinker at shortstop, but Frank Chance had already left for New York. The batter can't be seen behind the umpire and catcher, but you can just see his feet as he prepares to run to first.

Urban Clarence "Red" Faber
Career 1914–1933   Chicago 1914–1933

Red Faber went 254-214 with a career ERA of 3.15 and 1,471 strikeouts. He led the American League in ERA in 1921 (2.48) and 1922 (2.80). Faber was a lifelong White Sox pitcher, who pitched two full decades. His best years were 1915 (24-14, 2.55 ERA), 1920 (23-13, 2.99 ERA), 1921 (25-15, 2.48 ERA), and 1922 (21-17, 2.80 ERA). Faber was a spitballer, and the mediocre Sox teams he played for prevented him from joining the 300 win club. He learned the spitter in 1911, after a sore arm ruined a tryout for the Pirates. He had two sterling seasons for Des Moines of the Western League, and was signed by the White Sox after the 1913 season. Faber pitched for the 1917 White Sox World Series winners, going 3-1 with a 2.33 ERA for the champs, dominating the Series. He was inducted to the Hall of Fame in 1964.

CLAUD PRESTON "LEFTY" WILLIAMS
CAREER 1913–1920 WHITE SOX 1916–1920

Lefty, who would put together an 82-48 career on the south side, was just emerging as a dominant pitcher for the Sox in the late teens. In 1919, for the pennant winning Sox, Williams was 23-11 with a 2.64 ERA, his first 20-win season. Williams was one the eight men declared ineligible in 1920 for their role in the Black Sox scandal. Williams had a great season in 1920, his last, with a 22-14 record and a 3.91 ERA. Who knows what Lefty could have accomplished has he not be involved in the scandal. Lefty worked in a military shipyard in 1918, limiting the amount of games he played. Williams was the roommate of "Shoeless" Joe Jackson. He was inarticulate and moody. In the 1919 Series, the one he was accused of throwing, Williams had an 0-3 record and 6.61 ERA, after leading the league in starts and going 23-11 during the regular season.

BASEBALL
MAGAZINE

July   20c

Urban (Red) Faber getting ready to
put over one of his famous "spitters"!

Faber was the pitching star of the 1917 Series but missed most of 1918 and 1919 because of a stint with the Navy. He returned to help the Sox win the pennant in 1919. He didn't pitch in the Series due to a combination of the flu and a "dead" arm. His oddest feat came as a batter. A .134 lifetime switch-hitter, in 1915 he walked seven times in a row. He also stole home twice in his career. Faber also worked a few seasons as a White Sox coach and worked into his 80s as a surveyor for the Cook County Highway Department after he retired.

Arthur Neukom Nehf
Career 1915–1929 Chicago 1927–1929

Southpaw Nehf finished up a long and successful career with the Cubs. After pitching on four New York Giant World Series teams, Nehf had a couple of good seasons with the 1928 and 1929 pennant winners. Though he had solid career World Series statistics (4-4, 2.16 ERA) his two appearances for the Cubs in the big game didn't go so well (18.00 ERA). His last major league appearance came in Game Four of the 1929 World Series for the Cubs, where he failed to get anyone out. Nehf had 30 shutouts in his long career with the Boston Braves, New York Giants, Cincinnati Reds, and Chicago Cubs.

PHILLIPS BROWN "PHIL" DOUGLAS
CAREER 1912–1922 CHICAGO 1912, 1915–1919

"Shufflin' Phil" spent three seasons with the Cubs in the Teens, after making his debut with the Sox in 1912. Douglas was a spot starter for the Cubs in this period. He went 14-20 with a 2.55 ERA in 1917 for the Cubs and followed that up with a 9-9 record and a 2.13 ERA in 1918 for the pennant winning club. He picked up a loss in his only World Series appearance on an unearned run. Later in his career with the New York Giants, Douglas was banned by Commissioner Kenesaw Mountain Landis for discussing throwing a baseball game while he was hungover. After a taxing dry-out period and a relapse, and then a demoralizing tirade from his coach John McGraw, Douglas wrote a Cardinal outfielder about an ambiguous offer to quit on the Giants in the heat of the Pennant race in 1922, in return for an inducement. He was banned for life. When he was sober and his spitball was dancing, Douglas was one of the best right-handers in the National League.

CHARLES CULBERTSON "CHARLIE" ROBERTSON
CAREER 1919–1928 CHICAGO 1919, 1922–1925

You may be asking yourself why Charlie Robertson is in a book of aces with a 49-80 career record. Well, Charlie Robertson is the only pitcher in the history of White Sox baseball, as well Chicago baseball, to pitch a perfect game. No Cub has ever pitched a perfect game. He did it in his third major league start on April 30, 1922, against the Detroit Tigers. A diving foul line-drive catch by left fielder Johnny Mostil helped preserve the perfect game. He went 14-15 that season with a 3.64 ERA and followed that up with a 13-18 season and 3.81 ERA. Charlie's arm wore out in 1924 and he never fully recovered.

CLAUDE RAYMOND HENDRIX
CAREER 1911–1920 CHICAGO 1914–1920

Claude was one of a handful of players to end up with the Cubs after the Federal League folded before the 1916 season. Hendrix best season came as a Chicago Whale, when he dominated the Federal League in 1914, going 29-11 with a 1.69 ERA. He helped the Cubs win the pennant in 1918, when he posted a 19-7 record with a 2.78 ERA. He only pitched one inning in the Series, not allowing a run. He pitched a no-hitter on May 15, 1915, over Pittsburgh in a Federal League game. Hendrix's career ended suspiciously. The Cubs released him for supposedly betting against the Cubs in a game he was scheduled to pitch the previous August. He was replaced in that game by Grover Alexander.

1917 Chicago White Sox

The 1917 Sox won 100 games, mostly on great pitching and timely hitting. Happy Felsch knocked in 102 runs and batted .308 for this dead ball era club. Joe Jackson hit .301 with 75 RBIs. The pitching staff was led by Eddie Cicotte (28-12), Red Faber (16-13), Lefty Williams

(17-8), and the first prototype for a closer, Dave Danforth, who was 11-6 with nine saves, strictly in relief.

RICHARD HENRY "DICKIE" KERR
CAREER 1919–1925   CHICAGO 1919–1925

Dickie is best known for winning two games as a 26-year-old rookie in the 1919 World Series. He went 2-0 with a 1.42 ERA and 14 strikeouts in his two games against the Cincinnati Reds. Kerr followed up his success by going 21-9 with a 3.37 ERA in 1920, and 19-17 in 1921. He held out for a larger contract in 1922 and was suspended for the years 1923 through 1925. After pitching in a handful of games in 1925, his career was done. Kerr was the only honest starter the Sox had for the 1919 Series, throwing a shutout in one of his starts. After going 19-17 for a demoralized 1921 Sox squad, Charles Comiskey turned down Kerr's request for a $500 raise. Kerr responded by going to pitch for more money in the independent leagues. Kerr had a long career as a minor league manager. He is credited with converting Stan Musial from a pitcher to an outfielder. The Kerrs became friends with the Musials and Dickie Kerr was at the wheel when the first little Musial was born on the way to the hospital. The Musials named the boy Richard. When Musial achieved stardom with the Cards, he bought the Kerrs a house in Houston.

1920 CHICAGO AMERICAN GIANTS

This version of the American Giants finished last in the Negro National League with a 4-24 record. Notice the mish-mosh of uniforms. The players, from left to right, are: (front row) Bob Winston, Bob Anderson, unidentified, Joe Green, unidentified, Willie Green, and Jack Jennings; (back row) unidentified, Horace Jenkins, unidentified, unidentified, John Beckwith, Butler White, James Davis, and unidentified.

1926 CHICAGO AMERICAN GIANT PITCHERS

The pitchers for the World Champion American Giants, from left to right, are Webster McDonald, George Harney, Willie Foster, Rube Currie, Edward Miller, and Willie Powell. Other members of the staff, Aubrey Owens and Robert Poindexter, were not in this picture.

1919 CHICAGO AMERICAN GIANTS

Rube Foster is in suit and tie for the 1919 version of the Chicago American Giants. Pictured, from left to right, are (front row), unidentified, Jimmie Lyons, Bill Francis, unidentified, and unidentified; (middle row) Dave Malarcher, Bonny Williams, unidentified, and John Reese; (back row) Elwood "Bingo" DeMoss, Leroy Grant, Dave Brown, Rube Foster, Oscar Charleston,

and Richard Whitworth. Future Hall of Famer Oscar Charleston was a young player on this team. He went onto to play and manage the fabled Pittsburgh Crawfords Negro League teams of the 1930s.

CHARLES HENRY "CHARLIE" ROOT
CAREER 1923–1941 CHICAGO 1926–1941

After a brief stint with the Cards in 1923, "Chinski" jumped right into the Cubs rotation in 1926 and never looked back. Root went 18-17 with a 2.82 ERA in his first full season as a Cub, following that up with an excellent sophomore season leading the National League in wins, while posting a 26-15 mark with a 3.76 ERA. Root had 13 or more wins in 10 of his 16 seasons with theCubs. And each of his 102 career wins came in a Cubs uniform. Root didn't have much success in the World Series, going 0-3 with a 5.96 ERA in six games. He did pitch for four World Series Cubs teams though, in the late 1920s and early '30s. In 1969, Root was named the Cubs all-time right-hander. He was dogged later in his career because of Babe Ruth's "called shot" in the 1932 World Series. The tobacco squirting Root had always denied that Ruth made the called shot and said if he did, he would have thrown the ball at Babe's head. Root's version has Ruth lifting up a finger and saying, "I have one strike left."

John Duncan "Johnny" Rigney

Rigney was a career White Sox player. Johnny had a nice season in 1939, going 15-8 with a 3.70 ERA. He had two more productive seasons before he went off to war, going 14-18 in 1940 with a 3.11 ERA and 13-13 in 1941 with a 3.84 ERA. Rigney pitched the first night game at Comiskey Park in 1939. In 1941, he married the daughter of the team president and moved into club administration after shutting down his career due a sore arm. He eventually became Vice-President of the White Sox.

John Frederick "Sheriff" Blake
Career 1920–1937 Chicago 1924–1931

The Sheriff had a sub-par lifetime record of 87-102, but he did have some decent years for the Cubs. In 1928, he went 17-11 with a 2.47 ERA. He followed that up with a 14-13 record for the 1929 pennant winning Cubs. Blake appeared in two games for the Cubs in the 1929 Series, both in relief. He was the second of three pitchers in relief that failed to hold an 8-0 lead against the A's in Game Four. Blake took the loss when the A's scored 10 runs to overtake the Cubs, 10-8.

GUY TERRELL BUSH
CAREER 1923–1945   CHICAGO 1923–1934

"The Mississippi Mudcat" was an integral part to the pitching staff of the Cubs pennant winners in the late 1920s and early '30s. Bush won 15 plus games, seven straight years (1928-1934) and posted a 152-91 record as a Cub. Bush went 18-7 with a 3.66 ERA for the 1929 pennant winning Cubs and 19-11 with a 3.21 ERA for the 1932 pennant winners. Mudcat's best year was 1933, when he went 20-12 with a 2.75 ERA. Bush pitched in four World Series games. His best was the 1929 Series. The 'Cat' went 1-0 with a 0.82 ERA. He was traded to Pittsburgh in 1935 and gave up the last two home runs of Babe Ruth's career in a game against the Braves at Forbes Field. Guy Bush ran a tavern on Montrose and Western in the 1940s and '50s.

In 1939, manager Jimmy Dykes put Lyons (seen here to the right of Monty Stratton) on a Sunday-only pitch rotation to help save his arm and take advantage of the pitcher's popularity. This move continued through 1942, until he was off to the Marines.

In the fall of 1942, Ted (seen here on the left with Bill Dietrich), a lifelong bachelor, joined the Marines for a three year stint. He returned in 1946, and pitched five games for the Sox, winning his last game, giving him a total of 260 for his career. Some say the service cost him 300 victories for his career. He replaced Jimmy Dykes that season (1946) as manager. He was a failure (185-245) due to his lenient tendencies and lack of ability to dish out discipline when needed. He later coached and scouted until 1966. Lyons retired from ball to help his sister run a rice plantation in Louisiana.

Three

1931–1950

The years between the wars were good for the Cubs, and bad for the Sox. The Cubs would field competitive teams until 1946 before bottom fell out in the 1950s, with 1952 being the only year that Cubs were competitive at a record of 77-77. The Sox? Well, they were mired in mediocrity for most of the 1930s and 1940s, finishing somewhere between third and fifth during the Jimmy Dykes era. The Sox fortunes changed when Minnie Minoso and a young Ace, Billy Pierce, came to Chicago the early 1950s. The Sox did make it to the Series in 1959, 40 years after their previous appearance, and as of this writing it has been 45 years since their last appearance in the World Series.

The Cubs of the 1930s were the highlight of Chicago baseball. After appearing in the Series in 1929, the Cubs also made good showings in 1932, 1935 and 1938, following that up in 1945 for their last Series appearance, some 60 years ago.

Lon Warneke, Guy Bush, and Charlie Root, made up the staff for the Cubs Pennant Winners of 1932. They faced Babe Ruth again, but this time as a Yankee, and the Cubs were thumped four games to none. The Cubs staff in the Series had a 9.26 ERA.

In 1935, the Cubs won 21 games in a row at the end of the season to surpass the Dizzy Dean led Gashouse Gang (St. Louis Cardinals). Warneke, Larry French, and Tex Carleton were the Aces of this team that eventually lost to the Detroit Tigers in the Series, four games to two, behind Schoolboy Rowe and Rocky Bridges.

The Cubs faced the Yanks again in 1938, without Babe Ruth, but with a new Italian kid, Joe DiMaggio. The result was the same with the Cubs being swept in four games. Bill Lee, Larry French, Charlie Root and Dizzy Dean made up the rotation in the Series, which ended the same way as 1932, with the Cubs staff registering a 5.03 ERA for the Series.

In 1944, the Cubs brought back cherished manager Jolly Cholly Grimm, and soon the Pennant came back with him. In 1945, the Cubs played the Tigers and lost in seven games, 4–3. From living accounts, it was one of the worst played Series of all time. Both teams were chock full of 4-Fs from the Army and the play reflected it. Hank Borowy, Claude Passeau, and Hank Wyse led the staff that brought the Cubs to the brink of a World Series Championship. But a gamble by manager Charlie Grimm, bringing Borowy back to pitch Game Seven on one day's rest, backfired in the first inning and the game and Series was lost.

Hopefully the curse of the Billy Goat and the Black Sox take a hiatus soon. Next year, 2006, is the 100th Anniversary of the "L" Series. Maybe for the sake of Chicago baseball fans, this will become a regular one-hundred year occurrence, and we can see a World Series game in our lifetime.

Theodore Amar "Ted" Lyons
Career 1923–1946   Chicago 1923–1946

Lyons never pitched in the minor leagues, and never pitched in a World Series for two decades of nominal White Sox teams. Yet, through that, Lyons had the composure to win 260 games in his 20 year career. The Sox signed the young workhorse right out of Baylor University and he made his debut for the Sox soon after his graduation in July, 1923. In a game late in 1925, Lyons was on the winning end of a 17-0 win against the Senators, where he pitched a no-hitter up until two outs in the eighth inning. Lyons won 10 or more games in 17 of his 21 years for the White Sox of the Jimmy Dykes era. Ted led the American League in wins in 1925 (21-11) and 1927 (22-14). Lyons also posted a 22-15 record in 1930. He pitched a no-hitter August 21st, 1926, against the Boston Red Sox. Lyons was inducted to the Hall of Fame in 1955. In 1931, Lyons was declared to have a "dead" arm, usually meaning the end of a pitchers' career, but the crafty Lyons developed a knuckleball and pitched another 15 years. Lyons was not a strikeout pitcher, but had excellent control, once throwing 42 innings in a row without giving up a walk in 1939.

LLOYD VERNON "VERN" KENNEDY
CAREER 1934–1945 CHICAGO 1934–1937

Kennedy had his best seasons with the Sox in the late 1930s. His best season was 1936, when he went 21-9 for the Sox. Kennedy also pitched a no-hitter against the Cleveland Indians on August 31, 1935. In 1938, he suffered an arm injury while playing for Tigers and was traded to the Browns, where he combined to lose 20 games in 1939. The most amazing stat about Kennedy's 1936 season was that he led the American League with 147 walks versus 99 strikeouts and he still won 21 games.

Perce Leigh "Pat" Malone
Career 1928–1937 Chicago 1928–1934

After losing his first seven games, Malone popped on to the scene in his rookie season (1928) with a 18-13 record and 2.84 ERA—one of the best for any rookie pitcher in Chicago history. He followed that up for the 1929 pennant winners, by leading the National League in wins (22) and strikeouts (166). Malone also led the league in victories (20) in 1930. Malone didn't fare as well in the 1929 World Series, going 0-2 in four appearances, getting knocked out of Game Two in the fourth inning, and losing Game Five, 3-2. Malone was also slugger Hack Wilson's choice for a partner in crime. Malone and Wilson's benders enraged Rogers Hornsby who was the main reason both were shipped out of Chicago.

Thomas Alphonse "Tommy" Thomas
Career 1926–1937 Chicago 1926–1932

Tommy had double digit wins in his first four seasons with the Sox, going 15-12 with a 3.80 ERA in 1926, and posting a 19-16 record with a 2.98 ERA his sophomore season (1927). Thomas had a 32-12 record for the 1925 International League Baltimore Orioles, which caught the attention of Charles Comiskey. He became a workhorse for the Sox from 1926 to 1929; because of the overuse, Thomas couldn't get past the fifth inning by 1930. On July 24, 1927, Thomas gave up the first home run to clear Comiskey Park's new upper deck roof to Babe Ruth. Architects of the new addition to the stadium said it was technically impossible for a ball to be hit out of the park.

Lawrence Herbert "Larry" French

Career 1929–1942   Chicago 1935–1941

French, seen here during spring training on Catalina Island, was an integral part of the Cubs rotation for the pennant winning Cub clubs of 1935 and '38. French went 17-10 with a 2.96 ERA for the 1935 pennant winners and a dismal 10-19 with a 3.80 ERA for the 1938 Cub pennant winners. French's best season was 1936 with the Cubs, going 18-9 with a 3.39 ERA. Larry French won 10 or more games in 12 of the 14 seasons in his career. In the 1930s, only

Carl Hubbell pitched more innings than Larry French. The rugged southpaw appeared in 40 games each year for seven seasons. French also recorded 40 career shutouts. He ignited Chicago's 21-game winning streak in 1935, by winning five of the 21 games during the streak that clinched the National League pennant. He joined the Navy in 1943 and retired as a captain in 1969.

Jay Hanna "Dizzy" Dean
Career 1930–1947 Chicago 1938–1941

Dizzy Dean had the best years of his career with the Gashouse Gang of the 1930s in St. Louis. When the Cubs acquired him in 1938, Dean had been suffering from a dead arm in 1937. The 1938 season put him over the top and he never fully recuperated. Dean was 7-1 with 1.81 ERA before going down with an arm injury in 1938. As a Cardinal, Dean led the league in victories in 1934 with a 30-7 record and a 2.66 ERA and backed that up with a 28-12 season and a 3.11 ERA in 1935. He also led the league in strikeouts from 1932 to 1935, striking out between 182 and 199 batters in each of those seasons. Dean only had six seasons in the majors where he put up big numbers, but few pitchers had more accomplishments or shenanigans in such a short time. "Dizzy" was given his nickname by his Sargent in the Army, where he picked up the basics of pitching. He was pitching for semi-pro teams in San Antonio when he was discovered by the Cards. In 1930, he combined for a 25-10 Minor League record, his first season split between St. Joseph, Missouri, and Houston. Dizzy was called up in September and promptly pitched a three-hitter on the last day of the season. He pitched for Houston in 1931, where he struck out 303 batters on the way to a 26-win season. He was inducted to the Hall of Fame in 1953.

Dean won 18 games as a 21-year-old rookie for the Gashouse Gang in 1932. He also led the league in strikeouts, shutouts, and innings pitched that year. In 1933, he struck out 17 Cubs in a game, a record at the time. During spring training in 1934, Dean boasted that he and his kid brother, Daffy, would win 45 games between them. This seemed even more incredible because Paul (Daffy) had never pitched a major league game. Dizzy won 30 and Daffy won 19 that year, making them appear like visionaries. Dean (right) is pictured here with Gabby Hartnett.

Dean was narrowly beaten out by the Cubs' Gabby Hartnett (right) for the 1935 MVP. Dean's career took a downswing in 1937. After trying to sit out the All-Star Game due to exhaustion, he was begged by Cards owner Sam Breadon to appear in the game. Dean was hit in the foot by a line drive from Earl Averill. He tried to come back too soon before it was fully healed and altered his delivery, causing painful bursitis in his golden arm. He was traded to the Cubs before the start of the 1938 season for three players and $185,000. He replaced his blazing fast ball and dancing curve with a change up and slow curve. He only appeared for the Cubs in 13 games. He appeared in 30 games over the next three years. Dean retired at the age of 30 and became a broadcaster for the St. Louis Browns. In 1947, after frequent criticism of Browns pitchers, Dean took the mound three times, shutting out the White Sox for four innings on the last day of the season.

Dean's meteoric career provided reason to immortalize him. His bold tactics and braggart persona made an American folklore type out of Dean. He loved to bait opposing players before and during game. He bragged, but could easily back it up. He was a good gambler. Between Dean and Gashouse mate Pepper Martin, a prank could be had at any given moment in the

Cardinal clubhouse. His popularity and colorful approach to life followed him to the radio broadcast booth. His malapropism and blatant disregard for grammar were legendary, and the fans couldn't get enough of it. In 1950, when television was still a new invention, Dean began doing the "Game of the Week" on national TV. He remained in broadcasting for over 20 years.

LONNIE "LON" WARNEKE
CAREER 1930–0945   CHICAGO 1930–1936, 1942–1945

"The Arkansas Hummingbird" stepped into the Cubs rotation in 1932. After a couple of appearances the two years before, Warneke, in his first full season, posted some of the best numbers ever by a Cubs pitcher, going 22-6 with a 2.37 ERA. For the next four years Warneke was one of the best pitchers in the National League. In 1933, he was 18-13 with a 2.00 ERA. In 1934, he was 22-10 with a 3.21 ERA. In 1935, he was 20-13 with a 3.06 ERA, and in 1936 Lon was 16-13 with a 3.44 ERA. He was an All-Star in 1933, '34, and '36 for the Cubs. In five World Series appearances Warneke was 2-1 with a 2.63 ERA. During the 1935 Series against Tigers, he went 2-0 and a 0.54 ERA. He was traded to the Cards in 1937, where his singing and banjo picking gave him a place on the Mudcat Band, a clubhouse hillbilly band. Warneke no-hit the Reds on August 30, 1941. The Cubs paid $75,000 to get him back in 1942, but soon lost him to military service. After the war, Lon worked his way back to the game as an umpire.

CUBS ROOKIES ON HORSEBACK

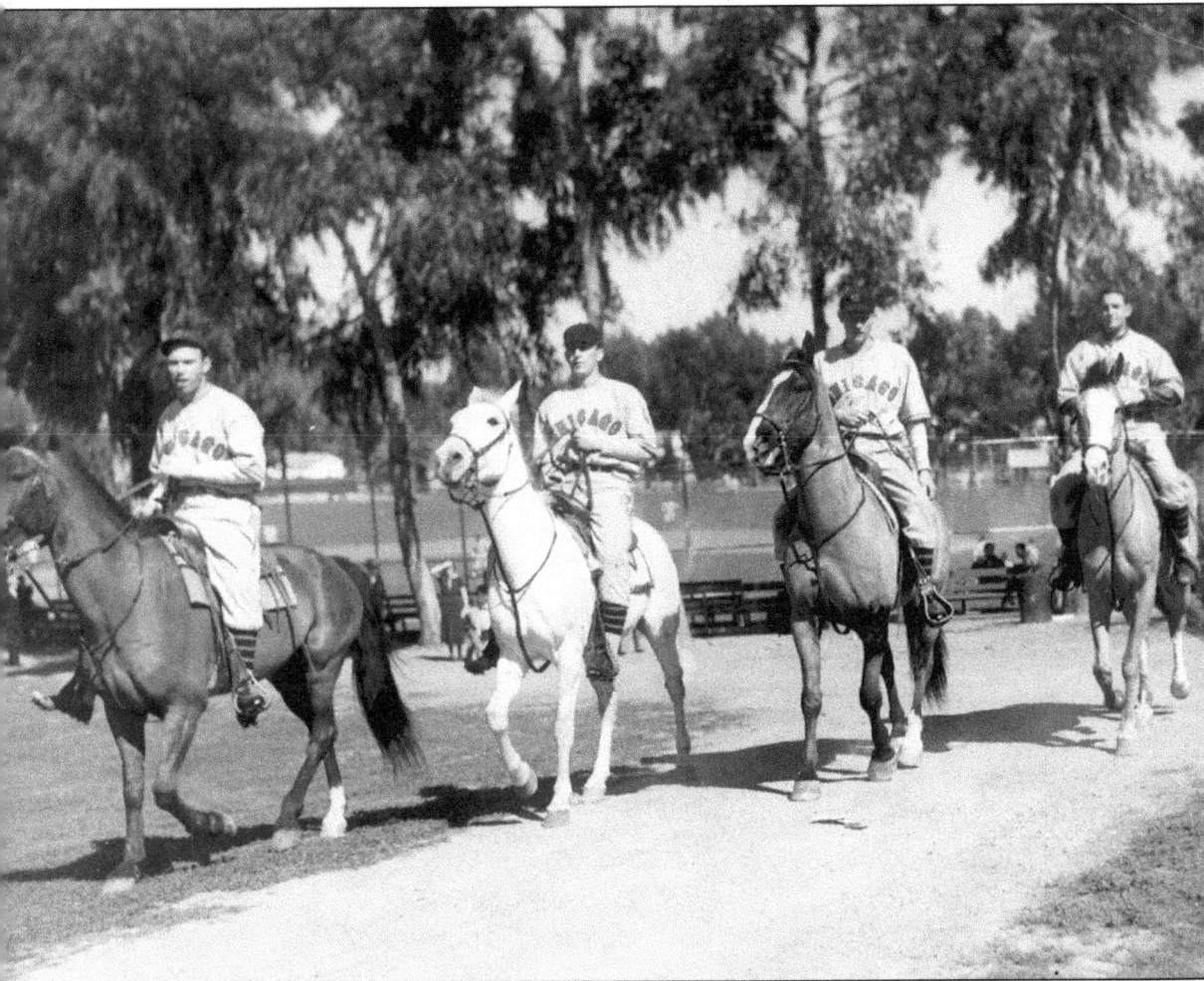

This is a charming picture of some young Cubs players horseback riding on Catalina Island. During the 1930s and 1940s, Catalina Island was the Cubs home for Spring Training. Spring Training in California was all the rage, until teams discovered the advantages of Arizona and Florida later in the 1950s and '60s.

PAUL DERRINGER

CAREER 1931–1945   CHICAGO 1943–1945

The "Duke" is another example of a career great pitcher that finished his career on a mediocre note in a Cubs uniform, getting all of his accolades elsewhere. Derringer was a four time 20-game winner for the Cincinnati Reds, before coming to the Cubs in 1943. After a couple of subpar seasons, Derringer was reborn in 1945, the last season of his 15-year career. Duke shook off the cobwebs and went 16-11 with a 3.45 ERA for the 1945 pennant winning Cubs. The Duke only saw limited action in the Series that year, appearing in three games and posting a 6.45 ERA. Before being sold to the Cubs in 1943, Derringer led the Reds to two successive pennants and the World Championship in 1940. He was also the winning pitcher in the 1940 All-Star Game and had two one-hit games that same season.

William John "Bill" Dietrich
Career 1933–1948   Chicago 1937–1946

"Bullfrog" threw a no-hitter in his first season as a White Sox pitcher, on June 1, 1937, versus the St. Louis Browns. Dietrich had a mediocre career after an arm injury affected him after the 1938 season. A journeyman and role pitcher for the rest of career, the White Sox always seemed to get the most out of Bullfrog. His best season with the Sox was 1944 when he went 16-17 with a 3.62 ERA. Unable to see without his glasses, Dietrich had a fireball for a fastball but never could harness his control. He didn't know he'd pitched a no-hitter when he did, because he had thought an error in the seventh was ruled a hit, which it wasn't.

1932 Chicago Cubs

Charlie Grimm replaced Rogers Hornsby as manager mid-way through the season and the team responded by catching and passing the Pittsburgh Pirates and winning the National League by four games. They were whipped in the Series by Babe Ruth and the New York Yankees. The

aces of this staff were Lon Warneke (22-6), Guy Bush (19-11), Charlie Root (15-10), and Pat Malone (15-17).

JAMES OTTO "TEX" CARLETON
CAREER 1932–1940   CHICAGO 1935–1938

Tex was a role pitcher for the Cubs pennant winners of the late 1930s. He was 11-8 with a 3.89 ERA for the 1935 pennant team and 10-9 with a 5.42 for the 1938 pennant winners. He lost his only start in a World Series game in 1935, but posted a 1.29 ERA. Carleton's best season was 1937 when he went 16-8 with a 3.15 ERA. Carleton pitched a no-hitter in 1940 as a member of the Dodgers.

ROY HENSHAW
CAREER 1933–1944   CHICAGO 1933–1936

The only good season of Henshaw's career was the 1935 pennant winning season for the Cubs. In his first full season as a pro, Henshaw posted a 13-5 record with a 3.28 ERA, helping the Cubs make the Series. Henshaw was hit pretty good in his only World Series appearance, sporting a 7.36 ERA. Henshaw was a graduate of the University of Chicago and it appears by this uniform and the background, it could be a picture of him while playing baseball in college.

JOHN HENDERSON WHITEHEAD
CAREER 1935–1942   CHICAGO 1935–1939

"Silent John" had four good seasons with the Sox at the start of his career, going 13-13 in 1935, 13-13 in 1936, 11-8 in 1937, and 10-11 in 1938.

THORNTON STAR LEE
CAREER 1933–1948   CHICAGO 1937–1947

"Lefty" was a rubber-armed southpaw who pitched for the mediocre Sox teams of the Jimmy Dykes era. Lee led the American League with a 2.37 ERA in 1941, going 22-11 that season, his best as a Sox pitcher. Lefty Lee posted double digit victories from 1937 to 1941. He broke his arm in 1944 and came back to win 15 games in 1945. An elbow injury in 1946 conspired to end his career. Lee was a rookie at the age of 27 for the Indians in 1933. Sox coach Jimmy Dykes liked what he saw in Lee as he struggled in Cleveland. Under the tutelage of Sox pitching coach Muddy Ruel, Lee blossomed as one of the top lefties in the league. In 1942, after posting his best season in 1941, Lee broke his arm and went under the knife for two bone chip removals and neck surgery. He was of little use for the next three years. In 1945, he bounced back with a 15-12 record. Lee pitched until he was 42, nine years before his son Don Lee, pitched with the Tigers. Ted Williams homered off of both of them, making him the only man to homer off of a father and son.

JOE HAYNES
CAREER 1939–1952   CHICAGO 1941–1948

The Sox got the most of Joe Haynes' career. He posted a winning record in his eight years in Chicago. Primarily a spot starter and reliever, Haynes best season with the Sox was 1947 when he went 14-6 with a 2.42 ERA. He was the Sox ace reliever in 1942, leading the league with 40 appearances, while going 8-5 with a 2.62 ERA and six saves. Haynes married Thelma Griffith, daughter of Washington Senator owner and former White Stocking, Clark Griffith. Haynes later became a Senators coach, general manager, and eventually vice-president. He is credited with moving the Senators franchise to Minnesota.

Randall Pennington "Randy" Gumpert
Career 1936–1952 Chicago 1948–1951

Gumpert was a journeyman pitcher who had one decent season for some bad White Sox teams. In 1949, Gumpert's only season in his career that he started over 20 games, Randy went 13-16 with a 3.81 ERA, starting 32 games. Most of career was spent as a reliever. As a teenager, Gumpert threw batting practice for the A's. His home was around Shibe Park. He eventually became a scout for the Yankees after his career was over.

Monty Franklin Pierce Stratton
Career 1934–1938   Chicago 1934–1938

"Gander" was just coming into his own in 1938 when his career was cut short by a hunting accident. In 1937, Stratton posted a 15-5 record with a 2.40 ERA. He followed that up with a 15-9 season in 1938. In 1939, White Sox management sponsored a Cubs versus Sox charity game with the proceeds ($28,000) going to Stratton. In a touching emotional moment, Stratton took the mound to show he could still pitch. After coaching for the Sox, he was given a minor league contract, and in 1946 he posted an 18-8 record in the East Texas League on an artificial leg.

Stratton (right), seen here with Jimmy Stewart, was called "Gander" because of the use of his trick pitch "The Gander." Stratton's major league career ended tragically at the age of 26. He was hunting rabbits when his gun discharged in November of 1938. The bullet lodged in his right knee and severed the femoral artery. His leg was removed the next day. Stratton's story was made into a movie starring Jimmy Stewart and June Allyson, *The Monty Stratton Story*. It was a box office smash in 1949.

CLAUDE WILLIAM PASSEAU
CAREER 1935–1947   CHICAGO 1938–1947

Four-time Cub All-Star (1941–1943, 1946) Passeau came from the Pittsburgh Pirates in the middle of the 1939 season. Claude made an instant impact by going 13-9 for the Cubs that season and leading the league in strikeouts with 137. In 1940, he had his best year as a Cub, going 20-13 with a 2.50 ERA. His next best season was for the pennant winners of 1945. Passeau was 17-9 with a 2.46 ERA for the Cubs that year. He also fared well in the World Series, going 1-0 with a 2.70 ERA in three appearances. In Game Three, Claude hurled a one hit shutout at the Tigers. Passeau lived inside with his pitches and was an emotionally competitive right-hander. Often asked about his uniform number 13, Passeau responded be saying, "That's my lucky number. My auto tag is 13. The serial on my rifle is 13. The last two digits on my life insurance is 13, and my address is 113 London Street." He also spent 13 years in the majors.

EDGAR "EDDIE" SMITH
CAREER 1936–1947   CHICAGO 1939–1947

The crafty southpaw Eddie Smith put together a good season in 1940, going 14-9 with a 3.21 ERA. It was his only winning season. He led the American League with 20 losses in 1942, posting a thin 7-20 record. Smith was a hardluck pitcher. Smith's ERA was consistently in the low to mid-threes. But an anemic Sox squad never garnered enough run support for the pitchers of the 1940s. Eddie was on the losing end of Bob Feller's opening day no-hitter in 1940.

1936 CHICAGO AMERICAN GIANTS PITCHERS

Pictured on the far left is famed curveball specialist Highpockets Trent. With his long curve, short curve, and shorter curve, Ted Trent won 45 games and lost 13 from 1936 to 1939. He

appeared in four consecutive Negro League All-Star Games (1934–37).

John Albert "Johnny" Schmitz
Career 1941–1956   Chicago 1941–1951

Two-time Cub All-Star (1946, '48), "Bear Tracks" pitched in the majors a total of 13 years, with mixed success. For the 1948 Cubs, Schmitz went 18-13 with a 2.64 ERA. It was the southpaw's only winning season as a Cub. Johnny led the league in 1947 with 18 losses, going 13-18 on the year. Schmitz also led the league in strikeouts in 1946. He was a noted Dodger killer, winning 18 games against them all time. Schmitz was eventually traded to the Dodgers along with Andy Pafko in 1951. Arm and shoulder injuries limited his effectiveness after leaving the Cubs. Schmitz got the name "Bear Tracks" by the way he shuffled to the mound.

CURTIS BENTON "CURT" DAVIS
CAREER 1934–1946   CHICAGO 1936–1937

"Coonskin" played little more than a year for the Cubs. After splitting the 1936 season between the Cubs and Philadelphia Phillies, Davis only played part of the 1937 season before an illness cut his year short. Davis was a steady pitcher. winning 10 games or more in 12 of his 13 professional seasons. His best year was 1939 with the Cards going 22-16 with a 3.63 ERA. As a rookie, Davis pitched in a league-leading 51 games, winning 19 of them for the 1934 Phillies. Davis was one of the players traded to the Cards for Dizzy Dean in 1938.

Hiram Gabriel "Hi" Bithorn
Career 1942–1947   Chicago 1942–1947

Hi Bithorn was a Cuban born pitcher for the Cubs during World War II. He posted an 18-12 record in 1944 with a 2.60 ERA, his best season in the majors. He also had seven shutouts to lead the league. After two years of military service, he ballooned to 225 pounds. He pitched mostly in relief, before being traded to the Pirates who released him. He pitched two innings for the White Sox in 1947, before a sore arm ended his career. Hiram Bithorn Stadium in Puerto Rico, where the Montreal Expos played briefly in 2003–2004, is named after this famed Cuban pitcher. Hi once threw a fastball at Leo Durocher's head in the opposing dugout. Durocher wouldn't stop jawing at him, so Bithorn decided to try and shut him up. Bithorn was killed in Mexico on New Year's Day, supposedly by the police for resisting arrest, while trying to make a comeback, pitching in the Mexican Winter Leagues.

WILLIAM CRUTCHER "BILL" LEE
CAREER 1934–1947   CHICAGO 1934–1943, 1947

"Big Bill" led the National League in wins in 1938 with a 22-9 record and a league leading 2.66 ERA for the pennant winning Cubs. Lee had double digit victory totals in each of his first six seasons as a Cub. His sophomore season (1935), Lee posted a 20-6 record with a 2.96 ERA for the Cubs pennant winners of that year. General Lee had a high legkick that deceived hitters and made it appear that his fastball had more speed. Mired in the Cards system, though successful, Branch Rickey decided to keep Dizzy Dean and trade Lee to the Cubs. Lee shut out the Phillies in his first major league start. In his dominant year of 1938, Lee had two substantial scoreless streaks. During one stretch Lee, pitched 32 scoreless innings, giving up one run over a 47 inning period, the only run coming from the bat of a pitcher. In September of 1938, he racked up another 37 1/3 scoreless innings. Lee lost his touch and his eyesight. His eyes began to fail to the point that he couldn't see the catcher's signals. With the help of eyeglasses, he went 13-13 in 1942, and then bounced around the league the next few years. After he retired, Lee underwent eye surgery for two detached retinas and eventually went blind.

Russell Charles "Russ" Meyer
Career 1946–1959 Chicago 1946–1948

The oft-injured "Mad Monk" began his 13-year career with the Cubs before going to play for the Phillies (1950) and Dodgers (1953 and 1955) World Series teams. His best season was with the pennant winning Dodgers in 1953, going 15-5. His temper preceded him, often yelling at umps for bad calls, and teammates for errors. Once with the Phillies, after being knocked out of a game, he took his spikes off and threw them at the shower ceiling. The force made the spikes stick. In June of 1955, he broke his shoulder in a collision and was never the same.

HENRY WASHINGTON "HANK" WYSE
CAREER 1942–1951 CHICAGO 1942–1947

"Hooks" had three good seasons for the Cubs of the 1940s: 16-15 in 1944 with a 3.15 ERA, 22-10 with a 2.68 ERA in 1945 for the pennant winners, and 14-12 in 1946 with a 2.68 ERA. In 1945, he lost a no-hit bid on April 27 against Pittsburgh. The Pirates Bill Salkeld singled with one out in the eighth to spoil the goose egg. Wyse didn't fair as well in the 1945 World Series, going 0-1 with a 7.04 ERA against the Tigers. He gave up a three-run homer to Hank Greenburg in losing Game Two. Hank was a sinkerball control pitcher. He suffered a spine injury that made him 4-F for the war, but he had to wear a painful back brace while he pitched.

HENRY LUDWIG "HANK" BOROWY
CAREER 1942–1951 CHICAGO 1945–1948

Hank came to the Cubs in the middle of the 1945 Cubs pennant drive from the Yankees, where he was 10-5. After being acquired for $97,000, he went 11-2 for the Cubs down the stretch. Borowy won two games for the Cubs in the 1945 Series, going 2-2. He shut out the Tigers in Game One of the World Series. He lost the fifth game and after pitching four scoreless innings in Game Six in relief, and getting the win, Cubs manager Charlie Grimm made the mistake of starting Borowy in Game Seven. After three consecutive hits in the first inning, Borowy was pulled and the Cubs went on to lose the game and the Series. During the remainder of this career, he was plagued by a sore shoulder and blister problems on his pitching hand.

111

William Robert "Bill" Wight
Career 1946–1958   Chicago 1948–1950

"Lefty" Wight had a nice year in 1949. The southpaw was 15-13 with a 3.31 ERA. The year before, 1948, Wight went 9-20. Lefty was a crafty thrower that gobbled up innings. He was a wild thrower. In 1948, when Wight was 9-20, he led the league in walks with 135 while striking out 68. As an unproven youngster in 1948, Wight was half way back from California to the Yankees spring training camp in Florida, when he found out he was traded to the White Sox, whose spring training facility was in Pasadena, California. He turned around and headed back West. Wight also has a dubious hitting distinction for futility. In 1950, Wight was 0-61 at the plate, for a .000 average, the lowest ever for anyone with over 50 at-bats.

SAUL WALTER ROGOVIN
CAREER 1949–1957   CHICAGO 1951–1953

Rogovin led the American League in ERA with a 2.78 ERA, when he was traded from the Tigers in 1951. He had a nice season in 1952, finishing 14-9 with a 3.85 ERA with the Sox. He struggled in 1953, before blowing out his arm. He took a couple of years off before giving it a shot again, but his comeback only lasted a couple of years as a spot starter and reliever. The sleepy eyed Rogovin started his career as a third basemen until shoulder troubles made him switch to pitching. Paul Richards worked on an overhanded delivery that got a few years more out of Rogovin. Rogovin was also reported to have fallen asleep on the bench on more than one occasion.

PAUL EDISON MINNER
CAREER 1946–1956 CHICAGO 1950–1956

Minner was a decent pitcher for some bad Cub teams of the 1950s. This crafty southpaw had a career best 14-9 season in 1952, sporting a 3.74 ERA, which was Minner's only winning season. He probably would have had greater success, if only he played for another team and not the Cubs. "Tall Paul" was the first pitcher to throw under the lights in a World Series in 1949 for the Dodgers. Minner tied for the league lead in losses in 1951, for the last place Cubs. Minner was a Cardinal killer going 21-8 against then lifetime. A severe back injury ended his career in 1956.

ROBERT RANSOM "BOB" RUSH
CAREER 1945–1960   CHICAGO 1948–1957, 1960

Rush was a hard luck pitcher for the hapless Cubs of the 1950s. Someone once said that Rush would have won 250 games if he hadn't played for the Cubs. Rush had a 17-13 record with a 2.70 ERA for the 1952 Cubs, the only Cubs team to hit the .500 mark in the '50s. Rush had the dubious distinction of leading the league in losses in 1950 with 20. Rush scraped up winning seasons in 1955 (13-11) and 1956 (13-10) before moving on the Milwaukee Braves, were he was able to get to the 1958 World Series with that team. He pitched nine games for the 1960 White Sox, before the end of his career. Rush had a long windup with a high kick. Rush was the winning pitcher for the National League at the 1952 All-Star Game.

1950 WHITE SOX PITCHERS

Pictured from left to right are Mickey Haefner, Billy Pierce, Bill Wight, and Bob Kuzava—a full

array of southpaws on the White Sox pitching staff of 1950.

Walter William "Billy" Pierce
Career 1945–1964   Chicago 1949–1961

Pierce, a seven-time White Sox All-Star (1953, 1955–59, 1961), was purchased from the Tigers for $10,000 and a backup catcher, Aaron Robinson. Pierce threw four one-hitters in his career. In 1953, Pierce threw seven shutouts and had a streak of 51 scoreless innings. On June 27, 1958, Pierce was one out away from pitching a perfect game, yielding a hit to Washington Senator pinch-hitter Ed Fitzgerald, who smoked one down the line. Billy Pierce was a hard throwing southpaw for the Go-Go White Sox. Pierce had double digits wins in eleven of his thirteen seasons with the White Sox. His 20 wins in 1957, led the American League. He also had 20 wins in 1956. Billy also led the league in strikeouts in 1953. Pierce had a hardluck season for the 1959 pennant winning Sox, going 14-15 with a modest 3.62 ERA. The Go-Go Sox were the modern version of the "Hitless Wonders," Pierce being the victim of low run production in his starts that year. During one of the Sox power outages, Nellie Fox turned to Pierce after they just scored a run and said, "Here's your run. Now go out there and hold it." If any pitcher deserves to get in the Baseball Hall of Fame that isn't already in, it is Billy Pierce. He has better career numbers then many currently in the Hall. His talent was right up there with Hall of Famers, Yankee Whitey Ford and Indian Bob Lemon. Billy did win a World Series game for the San Francisco Giants in 1962. He pitched in three games for the Sox in the 1959 World Series, all in relief, without giving up a run.

Howard Kolls "Howie" Judson
Career 1948–1954 Chicago 1948–1952

Judson was almost exclusively a reliever for some thin White Sox teams of the late 1940s and early '50s. Judson has one of the worst records ever posted in a White Sox uniform. In 1949, Judson posted a pathetic 1-14 record, as a spot starter and reliever. His .067 winning percentage that year is one of the worst ever in a season; he lost all 14 games in a row. After losing his first game in 1950, Hudson picked up a win in relief against the Browns to break his 15-game losing streak. Judson was known as a courageous man, pitching his final seasons knowing that he would eventually lose his eyesight due to a retina infection.

Leslie Fletchard "Bill" Fleming
Career 1940–1946   Chicago 1942–1946

Fleming was a career reliever in the 1940s compiling a 9-10 record for the Cubs in 1944. He led the league in 1944 with relief losses with 10. Fleming never returned to form after his stint in the Army. The curveball pitcher never seemed to live up to his stature at the minor league level, winning 18 for the Hollywood Stars in 1940, while leading the Pacific Coast League in strikeouts.

FRANK RICHARD PAPISH
CAREER 1945–1950 CHICAGO 1945–48

"Pop" was a lefty spot starter for the post-war White Sox. His best season was 1947 with a 12-12 record and 3.26 ERA.

DOYLE MARION LADE

"Porky" had a solid first full season with the Cubs in 1947, going 11-10 with a 3.94 ERA. He became a spot starter and reliever after that, and was out of baseball by 1950.

Frank Walter Hiller
Career 1946–1953 Chicago 1950–1951

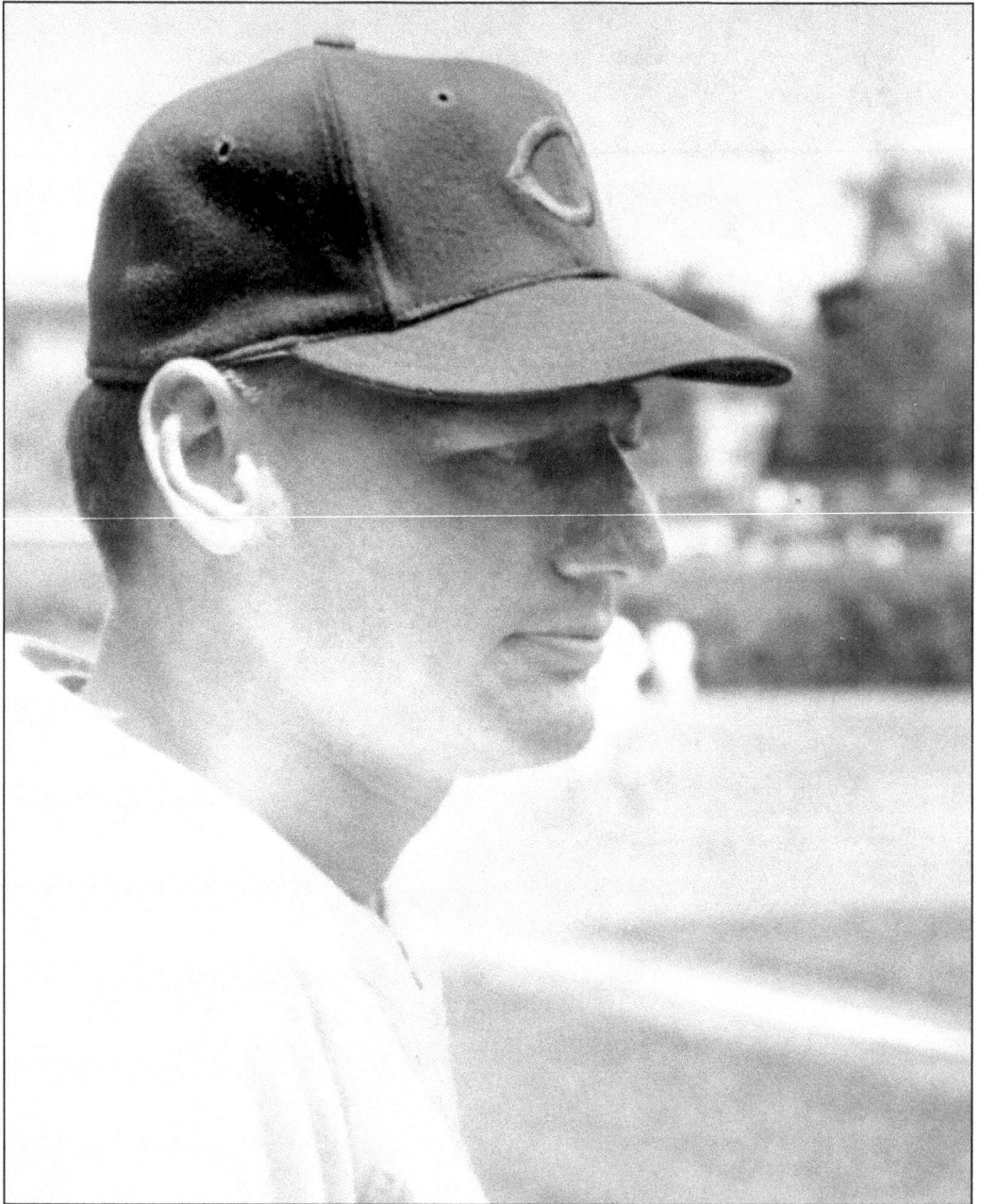

Dutch was a career spot starter and reliever. Hiller had a solid season for the Cubs in 1950, going 12-5 with a 3.53 ERA, the best of his career.

ROBERT MAX "BOB" CAIN
CAREER 1949–1953   CHICAGO 1949–1951

"Sugar" was a southpaw that had a decent year for the White Sox in 1950, going 9-12 with a 3.93 ERA. Cain went on the win 12 games the next two years for the Sox and Detroit Tigers. Sugar Cain was the pitcher when the famous midget Eddie Gaedel pinch-hit for the St. Louis Browns in 1951. He walked him, of course. His other noteworthy games were shutting out the Yankees in his first career start, and, in 1952, he matched one-hitters with Bob Feller, beating him 1-0.

OMAR JOSEPH "TURK" LOWN
CAREER 1950–1962   CHICAGO 1951-1962

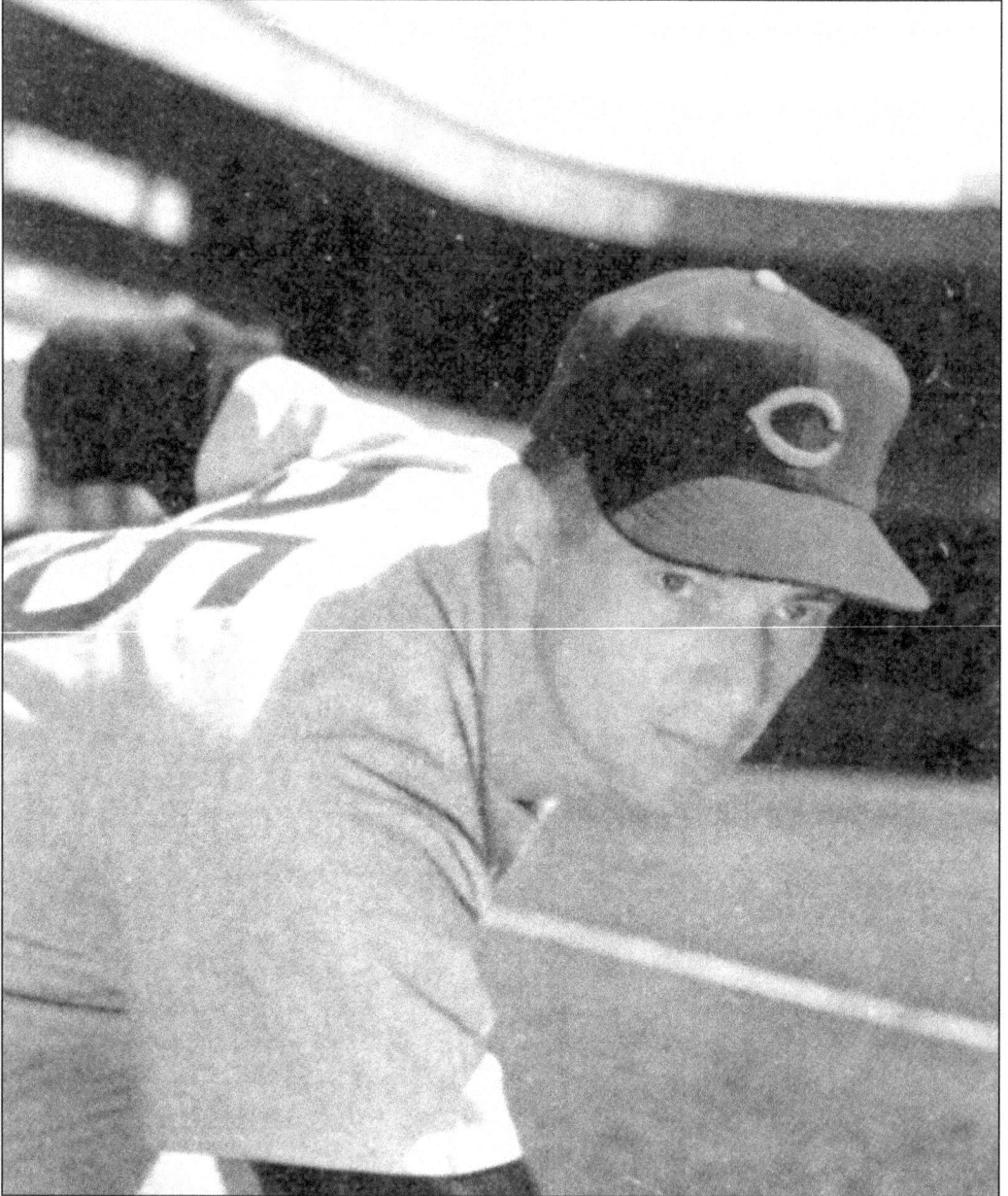

Turk had more success as a reliever for the White Sox, than as a starter for the Cubs. Lown was the earliest form of closer, just as the role started to develop in the mid-1950s, Lown developed with it. In 1959, Turk led all American League relievers with nine victories and 15 saves to help the Go-Go White Sox win the pennant that year. Lown was a wild thrower and got his nickname for his fondness for turkey.

POSTSCRIPT

The term "Ace" holds a special meaning in my heart. The word reminds me of my recently deceased father, Jack Freyer. He was not an Ace pitcher. He was an Ogden Ace, as in the Ogden Aces, the team of his childhood, at Ogden Park, in the Englewood neighborhood, on the Southside of Chicago.

Back in those days, and up until the day of his death, he was known as Stinky Freyer. Everyone that I ever met who knew my dad said he was the best athlete in every sport, not just one, including pool, ping pong, horseshoes . . . anything. The Ogden Aces was the name of his basketball team, football team, softball team, and soccer team as a kid. His sport of choice: 16-inch softball. Stinky has been nominated on occasion for the Softball Hall of Fame, but has never garnered enough support to get in. He also played for the Spalding Aces and his best friend and partner on the police department was Ace Powers, a fine softball pitcher in his day for the championship 4th District Chicago Police teams of the late 1960s, for whom Stinky also played.

My dad used to tell me that all he had to do from the time I could walk was give me a ball, and I would entertain myself for hours, throwing and catching the ball off the wall and steps. I started playing baseball when I was four (My mom lied to get me on my first team) and finished playing organized baseball when I tore my knee up in 1996 playing thirty-and-over ball—almost 30 years of baseball, of which I spent twenty as a pitcher.

I can thank my father for my hitting and fielding prowess as a ballplayer, but I had most of my success as a pitcher. I didn't learn a thing about pitching from him. I learned from another Ogden Ace, Stinky's older brother, Uncle Reggie.

When I was 12, my mom had breast cancer and survived, but we had to spend the summer at Uncle Reggie's house, while my dad worked three jobs. I had always heard stories that Reggie was a pro pitcher, or could have been, or the story about how he was shot in the knee in World War II, which ended his baseball career. To this day, I have never found out if any of this was true. Reggie passed in the early 80s, while I was in college. My other uncle, Ken, passed a few years ago. He was an Atomic War Hero, on the Montpelier, one of the first boats to land on Hiroshima, after the atom bomb was dropped. There is no one left to ask. Uncle Bob, the last of a great generation of Freyer boys, died in October 2004.

Like I said, I had heard stories about Reggie, so I asked him, once, if he could show me how to pitch. His face lit up. "Grab a catcher's mitt," he barked in his toughened firefighter tone, "meet me in the yard." Uncle Reggie had shoulders like a linebacker. Me? I was tall and scrawny, like Icabod Crane. He threw harder than anyone I have ever seen. His pitches danced in the wind, dropped off the table, and nailed me in the shins. I had only seen a ball go straight or curve a little, up until this point in my life. He spent the rest of the summer showing me pitching tips, but I think more than anything else, he loved to pitch. My older cousin, Kevin, was his receiver of choice, but he was in the Navy.

There's a special feeling that goes along with being a pitcher—the pop of the catcher's mitt, the look on the hitter's face when you drop a curve that makes his knees buckle. As a pitcher, you, like no one else, have complete control of the outcome of the game. I pitched for years and still yearn to strike out the side one last time. I figure Reggie had this same itch.

He taught me to hold the ball like an egg, not to hold it hard. He taught me the forkball, which is the same as the popular split-finger fastball used today. The main pitch he taught me, which is devastating to hitters, was the "disappearing fastball." It was hard to learn, but it worked like a charm. All he told me was, "Hold it as far back in your hand as you can, and throw." Sounds easy, but it's hard to control . . . once you did, batters would hurt themselves swinging at the pitch. After years of watching Greg Maddux pitch, I'd say his circle change is essentially a disappearing fastball.

After Uncle Bob's funeral, cousin Kevin and I stopped for a pint of the medicinal at a local Blue Island gin mill. We swapped stories about our fathers. I told him about my summer with Reg, while Kevin was in the Navy. "He must of loved that," Kevin said, "All Reg could ever think about was playing ball." Kev continued, "When we were little and living on Stony Island, I remember Reg standing on our porch and hitting fly balls all the way to St. Ailbe's." Uncle Reggie lived in a big apartment above an electric company on 92nd and Stony. The "porch" was actually the roof of a garage below. "He'd be out there hitting fly balls in his pjs and slippers to us in the school parking lot, we couldn't wait until he woke up on Saturday, within ten minutes, there were 25 kids out there pounding their mitts, trying to catch mile high fly balls," Kevin continued. To give you a sense of how far he was hitting the ball, St. Ailbe's was a good half-block away from the apartment. Reg was hitting the ball a good 400 feet, off of a roof.

I asked Kevin, if he heard any good stories about Uncle Reggie. He told me what he was told by my uncles and people that knew Reggie from the old neighborhood, that Reggie was the best pitcher around. He was playing for semi-pro teams at the age of 15, as a pitcher. Reggie would be picked up by teams that would play for blood money, sometimes in front of as many as 2,000 people at Ogden Park. Remember, these were the war years, the early 1940s, with no television, and neighborhood games were the entertainment. Thousands of dollars were waged in these games, the winning team getting a cut.

One particular story that drew my attention was that Uncle Reggie won a game 2–0 and struck out 15 when he was 15 in a semi-pro game. Reggie had pitched the whole game with a cigar in this mouth and a short beer on the mound. I've heard stories that he pitched a game in his socks, because he forgot his shoes, and pitched a shutout.

When I think of Aces, I think of the Ogden Aces. Reggie taught me how to throw the "disappearing fastball" that summer, and the forkball. After that, no one could hit me for a long time. This book is for Stinky and Reggie, the rest of the Freyer boys, and anyone who has ever been an Ogden Ace.

The Aces inside this book, the stories behind their careers, their pitches—the spitball, the shineball, the gander, the fade—all stirred up thoughts of Reggie, pitching with a cigar in his mouth. These Aces played ball when men were men and when whiskey and beer were the performance enhancers of choice. Like Stinky used to say, "There used to be iron tires and iron men, now we have rubber tires and tired men."

There are many iron-man pitchers in this book—Al Spalding, Ed Walsh, John Clarkson, Ted Lyons, Red Faber, Three Finger Brown, The Arkansas Hummingbird, and Rube Foster—with stories as colorful as American folklore.

The White Stockings, the Colts, the Orphans, the Cubs, the White Sox, the Whales, the Leland Giants, and the Chicago American Giants all had an ace or two on the staff. This book celebrates the men who have at one time or another dominated their league for a game, a year, or a lifetime.

John Freyer